T0041401

© Chris Bailey

Emily Carding (they/them) holds a BA (hons) in theatre arts from Bretton Hall and an MFA in staging Shakespeare from the University of Exeter. Having worked with tarot for over twenty-five years, Emily is the creator of several tarot decks, including *The Transparent Tarot* (Schiffer), and is author of *Faery Craft* and *So Potent Art* (Llewellyn) and illustrator of *Gods of the Vikings* (Avalonia Books). As an actor, they are best known for their international tour of the award-winning *Richard III* (*a one-person show*) by Brite Theatre. Emily lives in Hastings, East Sussex, England.

Seeking Faery

An Introduction to
the Hidden World
of the Fae

Emily Carding

Llewellyn Publications
WOODBURY, MINNESOTA

FIRST EDITION
First Printing, 2021

Cover and interior illustrations by Siolo Thompson
Cover design by Shira Atakpu
Interior design by Rebecca Zins

Llewellyn is a registered trademark of Llewellyn Worldwide Ltd.

LIBRARY OF CONGRESS CATALOGING-IN-PUBLICATION DATA
Names: Carding, Emily, author.
Title: Seeking faery : an introduction to the hidden world of the fae /
  Emily Carding.
Description: First edition. | Woodbury, Minnesota : Llewellyn Publications,
  2022. | Includes bibliographical references. | Summary: "*Seeking Faery*
  includes fascinating insights into the folklore and history of faery's
  magical beings and provides techniques for deepening your connection and
  developing honorable relationships with them"—Provided by publisher.
Identifiers: LCCN 2021036923 (print) | LCCN 2021036924 (ebook) | ISBN
  9780738766065 (paperback) | ISBN 9780738766386 (ebook)
Subjects: LCSH: Fairies.
Classification: LCC BF1552 .C375 2022 (print) | LCC BF1552 (ebook) | DDC
  398.21—dc23
LC record available at https://lccn.loc.gov/2021036923
LC ebook record available at https://lccn.loc.gov/2021036924

Llewellyn Publications
A Division of Llewellyn Worldwide Ltd.
2143 Wooddale Drive
Woodbury, MN 55125-2989
www.llewellyn.com

Printed in the United States of America

For my faery child,
who is no longer a child
but is ever faery

Contents

Exercises

And see not ye that bonny road,
Which winds about the fernie brae?
That is the road to fair Elfland,
Where you and I this night maun gae…
. . . .
Sir Walter Scott, "Thomas the Rhymer"

Introduction

The land and beings of Faery have long held fascination for us. Whether we were first captivated by ancient tales or modern portrayals, in Faery we see a reflection of truth that calls out to our hearts. We might not understand it at first, but a note of recognition is sounded, a spark is awoken deep within, and we may either choose to heed that call and follow the "bonny road" or keep that light buried and put it down to childish longings. That spark within thanks you for picking up this book, which will act as a guide to help you find your way to a deeper understanding and connection with Faery—or, at the very least, sate your curiosity!

Of course, most of us are raised in a culture that believes Faery is not "real," especially as we move into seemingly more and more materialistic times. We are told that our otherworldly cousins and the land they inhabit are the stuff of pure fantasy, and yet the deep truth that resounds through the ages in tales and encounters all around the world will not be denied. Our world and theirs need each other, now more than ever, and this book aims to help you make that connection whilst also being fun and informative.

What Is Faery?

"Faery" is an umbrella term for both the land and beings of a realm that exists alongside our own, hidden from everyday perception and yet intrinsically connected. The spelling of "faery" as opposed to the more familiar "fairy" is simply to differentiate between the powerful beings of the inner landscape and the more diminutive and disempowered creations of modern fantasy, but to quote Shakespeare, "A rose by any other name would smell as sweet"—and indeed, they may well present themselves to you by an entirely different name altogether.

The beings we may encounter that are encompassed by the label of faery are as infinitely variable as all life itself, from pixies and will-o'-the-wisps to the tall and noble Sidhe, from ancient gods to wizened gnomes, from tiny points of light to nameless beings as large as a mountain. To complicate matters further, these beings are often of so fluid a nature that our perception of them may be a combination of how they choose to appear and what our own psychological filters allow us to perceive. Through training and extending our senses and opening our hearts to their energy, we can hone our ability to perceive and communicate with them. This book will give you exercises to help build these skills and advise you on your continued development.

Why Faery? Why Now?

The human world is in disarray, having pulled further and further away from our intrinsic connection to nature. In an age of hot tempers, polarised opinions, bigotry, instant gratification, and mass consumerism, we are in dire need of renewed allyship with the unseen powers of the inner world. We need their help to slow down, reconsider, and reconnect our hearts to timeless truth.

The landscape of Faery is vivid and ageless, where all time exists at once and the energetic template of existence is unsullied by entropy and so-called progress. Faery is often described as being the other side of a veil or within the hollow hills, and though this draws obvious parallels with the land of the dead (and we will look at how the two are connected), Faery is much more a source of primal life, creation, and renewal.

To visit and work with Faery is to connect with the roots of existence and drink from the healing waters of the Grail. To work on strengthening our connection with the land of Faery is to not only enrich our own inner life but to benefit both worlds, for there is work to be done there that they cannot do without us, and there is work to be done here for which we need their collaboration. We share a world, existing within it on different resonances, and though there are those among the fae who would rather have nothing to do with us, there are many who see collaboration and partnership with humanity as a path to wholeness and healing of our world. Our short-sightedness is as damaging to them as it is to us, but they need us to open our awareness and reach out to them in order to do the work that must be done.

Your Guide

My own journey with Faery goes back as far as I can remember, though my first visits to the realm were not conscious and it was not until later in life when I realised the significance of those early experiences. As a child I had regular dreams of a wooden door in a hill that would appear in my garden, slightly ajar, with light behind. I would travel through the door, down into the hill, and emerge into a magnificent and vibrant realm full of mythic beings. Sometimes these beings would give me missions that I needed to perform for them; sometimes I would face tests and challenges.

In my late teens and early twenties, I started to explore more seriously, with especial interest in Celtic and Arthurian mythology alongside an instinctive magical practice. I trained as an actor at a drama school called Bretton Hall, which was on the grounds of a nature reserve in West Yorkshire, UK, and spent more time sitting in trees and connecting with the spirits of place than I did in my classes, much to the chagrin of my tutors!

After a few years of working as an actor, I became pregnant. I redirected my creative energies towards the esoteric for several years, including creating *The Tarot of the Sidhe*, which acts not only as a divination system but as a bridge between worlds. I studied with renowned teachers such as Caitlín and John Matthews and R. J. Stewart and artists such as Brian and Wendy Froud.

In 2012 my book *Faery Craft* was published. It is around this time that I revived my theatre career by undertaking an MFA in staging Shakespeare at the University of Exeter, and since then my life has been a weaving together of all these threads, always informed by my spiritual and magical practices. I was fortunate enough to spend many years of my life living rurally in Yorkshire, Cornwall, and Devon. I now live in a town on the southeast coast of England, and I hope to inspire those who live in urban environments as much as rural to seek connection with Faery, for truly its presence may be felt in cities as well as in the countryside. It's only that there's more noise and busy human energy to filter out to sense the truths beneath.

How to Use This Book

Seeking Faery is an easy-to-use guide to connecting with the realm and beings of Faery that you can carry with you anywhere. You won't need anything except the book itself, though there may be suggestions for extended practices or activities that you can choose to act upon as you wish. It contains a mixture of knowledge (in easy bite-size chunks) and practical exercises throughout that can enrich your life and help open you to the energies of the otherworld. Though this book is aimed primarily at beginners, it will appeal to lovers of Faery at all levels of experience as it is small enough to be kept always in a handbag or pocket and readily dipped into for inspiration. You may either work methodically through the book sequentially or dip in and out as you wish.

The Road Ahead

We begin our journey in the first chapter with a look at the nature of the Faery realm and its inhabitants, including the vast variety of beings that may be called faery and our relationship with them. We'll ask why we should be working with faery beings today and practice opening ourselves to the energies of the inner earth.

In the second chapter we'll go deeper into the history of Faery, from ancient myths and folklore, including Celtic and Arthurian legends, to accounts of actual encounters. We'll look at a number of historical figures who are connected to Faery and see what we can learn from their legacies. We'll see how our perception and portrayal of Faery has evolved over the centuries and explore how we can discern the underlying truths beneath interpretation. We'll take a guided meditation to meet a key faery being from mythology and learn how the wisdom they offer is very real.

In the third chapter we'll take this experience further and look at the many different ways we can extend and expand our senses in order to encompass a deeper level of being and connect with Faery. This will include exercises in visualisation, journeying into an image, using a symbol as a gateway, and taking an underworld journey to meet your faery ally.

The fourth chapter takes you into the heart of the sacred landscape, giving you guidance on how to best connect in those places where the worlds overlap.

Chapter five supports us in our journey to develop the connection further, with important notes on Faery etiquette and how we can live in harmonious relationship with our inner allies in daily life. We'll look at the practice of leaving offerings and the reasoning behind it, as well as how the world of Faery overlaps with our own environment, be it rural or urban. There will also be guidance on shrine building for those who wish to dedicate themselves more intensely to the Faery path.

The sixth chapter looks at how Faery relates to our own creativity and how connecting to Faery may unlock inspiration. We'll explore the power of voice as a means of energetic expression and connection, and we'll look at the ways in which many people have expressed their devotion to Faery through art and poetry.

In chapter seven—seven is an important number in Faery—we'll journey through the year and look at times when it is traditionally easier to pass between realms, as well as the concept of Time and Faery, which can be tricky! There will be suggestions for activities during the key festivals throughout the year and the different cycles of the moon.

Each chapter ends with a tale taken from the myths or folklore of Celtic lands, specially chosen to illustrate the lessons in the book and to strengthen the imaginative engagement with the material. Stories such as these are the means by which deep truths are conveyed, and spending time in contemplation of these tales will aid in unlocking the mysteries of Faery.

We finish with a blessing to send you deeper on your journey.

For now, we stand at the threshold of that journey—the first steps, perhaps, of a dance. A door before you opens, a figure holds out a gentle hand...will you take it and step through?

Come away, O human child!
To the waters and the wild
With a faery, hand in hand,
For the world's more full of weeping
than you can understand…

. . . .

W. B. Yeats, "The Stolen Child"

Seeking Faery

Faery is as vast and various as nature itself and full of contradictions. Both the land and beings of Faery are of a nature so in-between all that is that they defy exact definition despite our best efforts, being about as easy to pin down as it is to capture liquid light in a glass vessel. Nevertheless, we shall persist and do our best to look at the different categories of being, knowing that any attempt to define them can only show one facet of a shifting multidimensional form.

Defining the Undefinable

When we consider the true nature of the land of Faery and its inhabitants, we must take into account our sources and influences, as well as the very nature of our perception of truth itself. That might sound like a bit too much for an introductory level to a subject, but bear with me—it's not as complicated as it sounds.

All matter in the universe is actually energy vibrating at different frequencies that creates the effect, or illusion, of solidity. When we have an encounter with a faery, we are perceiving a being that is vibrating on a different frequency from our own, whose form is not as fixed as ours, and who may choose to appear to us in a particular way, or whom our brain will perceive differently according to the sum of our experiences and knowledge to that point. Therefore, young children with open perception and no reason to question the nature of what they are perceiving, nor much knowledge nor experience to inform their senses, find it easiest to encounter faery beings in the form they are choosing to present themselves in or in a pure energy form. As adults in the modern age, we are conditioned to engage the world in a solely rational way, and the very act of existing on our frequency, often surrounded by the everyday challenges of towns and cities and the background noise of others' lives, makes it more difficult for us to be open to the existence of otherworldly beings, even when we seek them out. Hence those who do not believe in the reality of beings beyond our own frequency are unlikely to perceive them at all.

You'll notice I do my best to use "perceive" rather than "see." This is partially to avoid an ableist attitude and acknowledge that we all experience the world through our senses in different ways, but it's also to address the issue that many people get so caught up in a desire to "see" faeries, with a fixed idea of what that means, that they are not open to using their full scope of energetic sensitivity. It is through empathic and holistic means we receive the signals that may or may not be interpreted by the brain into an eventual visual image. We will address this issue later in this chapter, but first let's look at our current understanding of the beings of Faery, which comes from a combination of myth, folklore, and the experiences of Faery seers and visionaries, all of which inform each other.

Hierarchy

Just as light exists both as a particle and a wave, so Faery hierarchy may be seen as both a pyramid structure and something more like a Russian doll, with smaller beings existing within larger ones.

Renowned Faery seer and author R. J. Stewart describes Faery hierarchy as starting with

> huge beings who are of, say, the Atlantic or the Pacific, or of the European land-mass…which is what the Greeks would have called Titans. Inside them you have lesser (but still very large) beings that are of the mountains or forests…Then eventually, just as in the human world, you get the smaller inhabitants who live in that region, the difference being that these are all consciousness (Carding 2012, 27).

Whilst there is also a very clear hierarchy that takes on a more traditional structure, it's possible that this is either a mimicking of human society or simply how our brains interpret the energetic signature of the beings in question. Whichever is the case, it gives us a strong structure to categorise the different classes of being we may encounter without going into a full dictionary listing of every sprite from folklore.

Titans and Giants

Most people think of small winged beings when they think of faeries, and far fewer folk will think of the ancient beings known as Titans who are as large as an ocean or a continent. This name hearkens back to the ancient Greek myths of the primal forces that reigned over the earth before they were overthrown by the Hellenic pantheon, and they are the living forces within the earth who are connected deeply to the forces of creation, destruction, and regeneration. Just as it is difficult for us to be truly aware of the entirety of our city at once, let alone the whole landmass, so we may not perceive the presence of these beings unless we purposefully meditate on their natures.

Whereas Titans are so large as to be quite removed from the span of human existence, giants, on the other hand, have frequently dealt with humans. They are profoundly wise guardians of mountainous and remote areas and have been known to take on a kind of mentoring role with those who prove deserving.

Faery Queens and Kings

Faery queens and kings are either powerful beings who rule over particular geographic areas and any other beings within those areas or they are ancient goddesses or gods who count faery queen/king as one of their titles and functions. Many are familiar with the concept of a queen and king of Faery from Shakespeare's A *Midsummer Night's Dream*, but Titania and Oberon existed well before his play.

Titania is a name taken from Ovid's *Metamorphosis* and is one of the titles of the goddess Diana. Diana has long counted queen of faeries amongst her many roles, and other goddesses also carry this title, such as the Morrigan and Hekate. It is thought that Oberon is taken from a German text; however, variations of the name also appear in Renaissance grimoires, and it's uncertain which came first.

Unlike other spirits of the grimoires, faery queens and kings will not be commanded but rather appeased. They are able to cross any magical barriers that human magicians employ and are very protective of the areas over which they are guardians. They are great appreciators of art, song, and poetry as offerings.

The Sidhe

Originally a Scots and Irish Gaelic name for a powerful race of beings (whose origins and history we will explore further later in the book), the Sidhe (pronounced *shee*) is a name often used to encompass all of Faery and refers to both the beings and the mounds in which they dwell. However, it is also the name used by powerful inner-world guardians who are a race distinct from what we might more accurately refer to as "nature spirits."

As experienced by modern mystics such as myself and many others (including John Matthews, author of *The Sidhe: Wisdom from the Celtic Otherworld*, who discovered the Great Glyph of the Sidhe, which we will use later), the Sidhe are powerful, noble beings intent on working with humanity to bring about our evolution and help save the planet we are both part of.

They take on forms that connect to our understanding of their Celtic origins, but their truth is closer to shifting forms of light that have descended from the cosmos into our world. They are shards of the divine, closely related to the concept of anima mundi, or world soul, with whom we can communicate and collaborate to restore balance to our lives and the earth.

Trooping Faeries

"Trooping faeries" is a term used to refer to the Faery nobility, and there is some overlap here with the traditional understanding of the Sidhe, who have been given their own section above to distinguish the beings of recent mystical explorations. They are so called because they tend to appear in groups, sometimes seen processing across the land and engaging in what appears to be mimicked activities and ceremonies of human society. Because of this they are sometimes confused for spirits of the dead, as they tend to appear in clothing that is one or two centuries out of date.

Other names for trooping faeries are lords and ladies, the lordly ones, and the gentry. They often appear armed and can have a military bearing. It is not wise to cross any faery being, particularly the trooping faeries, as they are powerful and can be ruthless.

Nature Spirits

Many of the other categories could be considered nature spirits, and it may be argued that all faery beings come under this category. However, there is some distinction to be made between independent beings who may travel as they wish and those who are connected to a particular landmass, hill, or tree, and there is also a distinct difference between the Faery nobility and, say, the spirit/dryad of an oak tree or the nymphs and naiads that might be found around water. It is a very wide category that includes beings of such wondrous variety of size and appearance as nature itself.

Nature spirits will usually display traits strongly connected to one element (earth, air, fire, or water) but do not consist solely of that element. They are most easily contacted in the wild places that are unfrequented by humanity, but they exist wherever you may find life—from a cactus in the desert to a weed poking through a crack in a sidewalk to the heights of a mountain range and the depths of the ocean. Connections with local nature spirits can be built through regular offerings and maintaining the spaces in which they dwell.

Genius Loci

The term *genius loci* originates in ancient Roman culture and means "spirit of place." There's obvious overlap with a couple other categories here, and spirits of place will include any nature spirits of trees, plants, and water in the area. They are the guardians of particular geographic locations and vary in size and powers. They should be appeased by asking for blessings and giving them offerings before any magical working is attempted outdoors; indeed, it doesn't hurt to have them on your side when engaging in any nonmagical activity either!

Elementals

Each of the four classical elements—earth, air, fire, and water—have elemental beings, which are the spirit of this element in its purest form. These are called gnomes, sylphs, salamanders, and undines/ondines/nereids, respectively. Mostly these will not be encountered

in nature, as all elements in nature require combination with other elements to sustain themselves. There are certain nature spirits that may resemble them, however, which may be much more frequently encountered. As spirits of the purest building blocks of life in action, elementals will either be encountered where these primal forces are most active or be conjured or created by magical practitioners.

Solitary Faeries

Solitary faeries (a term coined by the poet and visionary William Butler Yeats) are folkloric faeries of individual character and motivation. They often seem disconnected from a sense of tribe, hive mind, or community (though there are always exceptions, such as the banshee with its strong ancestral link) and do not generally seek interaction with humans unless it is antagonistic. They usually appear in forms that humans do not find appealing. The most tricksy of spirits, such as the pooka and leprechaun, could be placed in this category.

Domestic Spirits

There is a strong folkloric tradition of faery beings who are particularly connected to households and farms, often performing domestic tasks at night when the human inhabitants are sleeping. The best known of this kind of spirit in British folklore is the brownie, and if you find your unfinished housework all completed for you in the morning, be sure to pay your faery helper with a dish of cream or milk, otherwise they may become more inclined to mischief! These domestic spirits, like many faery beings, are the spiritual descendants of old gods. Many cultures around the world had gods of the hearth or ancestral household deities, such as the Lares of ancient Roman society, who were invited to share meals as though they were part of the family.

Unseelie

In Scottish lore, the faery race is split between those friendly to humanity—the Seelie court—and the Unseelie court, who would prefer we didn't exist at all. In Nordic culture there are the elves of Alfheim and the dark elves of Svartalfheim. All cultures around the world with a tradition of faery beings have their equivalent malevolent beings, and it is best to leave these well alone. If we consider our track record in regard to our treatment of the planet and our keeping of promises, it is little wonder that there are beings of this kind that wish no dealings with us.

Faeries and the Dead

Throughout folklore, there has always been significant overlap between the realm of the dead and the realm of Faery. After all, the Sidhe are named for the very mounds in which the ancestors were buried; West Country tradition states that unbaptised human children became faeries when they died; and when trooping faeries appear much like marching soldiers, wearing clothing that looks like uniforms from past eras, it is easy to see how the two could be confused. When we consider the fluid nature of Faery, perhaps we should also consider that it will always be difficult not only to define them but also to define the boundaries between them and other otherworldly forces. Sometimes answers are both yes and no at the same time, and while we remain limited by our own corporeal form and linear thought patterns, it may be futile to think we could fully understand where those boundaries lie.

There are folkloric accounts of people encountering the shades of those thought deceased, only to have them explain that they had eaten of faery food and hence became trapped there. There are also those who worked closely with Faery throughout their lives and now may be encountered as emissaries between the worlds, such as Reverend Robert Kirk, author of *The Secret Commonwealth*. The connection is clear and the distinctions are difficult to make, but the clearest way to state it is that the land of the dead and the land of Faery are different layers of what we might call the underworld, and that though we may encounter spirits of the dead within Faery, faery beings themselves have never been human. They precede us and will exist long after humanity has passed.

How to See Faeries

We live in a very visual-oriented culture, so it is only natural that many people's first question when they are seeking to connect with Faery is how to *see* faeries. However, sight is only one of our senses. Our eyes can deceive us, and also our eyes are designed to see what is physically in front of us, not to truly interpret signals that may be on a different frequency. When people talk of seeing faeries or other spiritual beings, it is rather that a combination of the mind, soul, and psychological filters derived from all our knowledge and past experience combine to form an impression that is interpreted into a visual and/or auditory perception.

If we get too caught up in the idea of seeing faeries, there's a danger that we will trick our brains into creating an illusory experience in order to satisfy the longing—or, more often than not, that we

block what innate ability we might have to sense them by dwelling too much on the one sense. When we truly perceive Faery, it is not through our eyes but through the whole self, and our first step in honing that ability must be in keeping a true and open heart.

Becoming the Faery Tree

This exercise is designed to connect you to the energies of the land and open up your heart centre to increase sensitivity to the presence and communications of faery beings.

Depending on your physical capabilities, this may be performed standing or sitting. In either instance, ideally you should have your feet bare and directly on land outside, in as natural a space as possible, where you won't be disturbed. Keeping upright and relaxed, with your feet a small distance apart and your hands by your sides, take seven slow, deep breaths in through the nose, hold for three seconds, then slowly out through the mouth as you allow tension and concerns of the day to melt away.

On your next breath, with your palms at your side facing downwards, imagine your feet slowly turning into tree roots and digging down into the earth beneath you. Feel the strength of the earth and the stability and nourishment that the roots provide you with. Maintain this for seven deep breaths in and out.

Now, for your next seven breaths, maintaining your roots, slowly bring your arms up into a V shape and raise your palms to the sky. Imagine that your arms are becoming great branches, reaching for the light of sun, moon, and stars. Maintain both roots and branches for a further seven deep breaths.

Keeping your arms upright in the V position, now imagine that your roots are drawing emerald green light up from the earth towards your heart. Breathe it in and draw it up with seven deep breaths. Now imagine that your branches are drawing down the silver light of the heavens into your heart. Draw it down with seven deep breaths. The green and silver lights meet in your heart and become golden and swirling, opening your heart to the energies of earth and connecting you to above and below.

For beginners, maintain this as long as you are comfortable and then release the energies back up through your branches and down through your roots, slowly lower your arms, draw your roots back into your feet, and become your normal self again. Take seven deep breaths to recover. As you become more used to this exercise, you may find you can do shorter or longer versions as you wish.

For more advanced practitioners, you may experiment with extending this golden light into the space around you in order to connect with other parts of the natural world. Guidance on a more advanced use of this technique may be found in the Walking in Awareness exercise. You may also combine this with the Freeing Your Voice exercise and use your voice together with the golden light to reach out. Then draw the light back into your centre and release back to above and below, following the same closing steps as above.

It is a good idea to maintain this exercise as a regular practice, and if you are hoping to connect with a particular area, this is a good way to open yourself to the energies of the space and introduce yourself to any beings that might be present and wishing to connect with you, especially when combined with the Freeing the Voice exercise. Spend some time in quiet contemplation in the area you have been working in after doing this exercise and see what impressions or beings come to you. It's all about being open and receptive without preconceived ideas of what might happen. An open heart is your gateway into Faery.

The World Soul

There are various myths, such as the Babylonian Inanna or the myth of Lucifer (which means "light-bringer"), in which a divine energy falls into the regions below the earth from the heavens above. In the case of the fall of Lucifer, this directly connects with the origins of Faery in Irish folklore, as it was said that those angels who were swept down with Lucifer in the Fall but did not wish to go to hell remained in the hollow places of the earth. These tales are symbolic ways of explaining how spiritual energy descends from a universal source in order to enliven and ensoul matter and beings on earth, then is radiated outward again in a repeating cycle of renewal. This descent of spirit into matter and the various myths that tell this tale connects to the Neoplatonic concept of the world soul, or anima mundi. As radiant guardians of the inner earth, faery beings are an intrinsic part of this process, and the realm of Faery is the primal core of the earth through which spirit is renewed.

The World Soul Meditation

Either stand, sit, or kneel comfortably in a place where you will not be disturbed and you can have a candle burning safely. Any candle will do, even a tealight, so long as it is in a safe holder. It is the flame that is important.

Place the candle before you. Take three deep breaths, releasing all the worries of the day with each breath out, and then light your candle.

Take three more deep breaths as you sit and observe the light from the candle.

Keeping your breathing steady, be aware of the rays of light touching you and how its energy becomes part of your energy field. Stay with this awareness for three more breaths.

Expand your awareness to other things touched by the light. You are all connected by these rays of light. Hold this awareness for another three breaths.

Now imagine there are no barriers between the light of the candle and all you can see. It is all touched by—and connected by—this energy. Contemplate this for three breaths.

How far can you visualise this connection spreading? Become aware of the light of the candle as a great pillar of light that stretches both to the beyond, above and out of vision into infinity, and down into the below, out of sight and beyond awareness. It expands in all directions beyond limit and connects everything it touches with the same illuminating energy, with no diminishing over distance or time. The light from the candle flame travels between worlds. It enlivens and ensouls all.

Closing your eyes, imagine that the candle exists within your solar plexus, or your centre. Feel how the energy connects to all things, as if you are at the centre of a great web. Expand this awareness as much as you are able to, taking all the time you need.

As you expand this awareness, become aware that all living things have their own candles at their centres, sparks of the same great light, a pillar that extends from above to below and from below to above in a continuous flow and renewal of life force, of soul. Hold this awareness for at least three breaths.

When you feel it is time, slowly withdraw your awareness a stage at a time, taking three breaths again at each stage. Feel your awareness returning to yourself and the space you are in, but retain knowledge of the connection.

Open your eyes and return your awareness to the candle flame.

Take three deep breaths, knowing your internal flame is ever lit. You may extinguish the candle when you are ready.

The Land of Faery

The land of Faery goes by various names. In Ireland it is Tír na nÓg, or land of the ever-young; the romantic Arthurian tradition calls it Avalon, and Scottish lore simply calls it Faireland or Elfhame, which has obvious parallels with the Norse Alfheim. Modern practitioners often refer to it as the Celtic otherworld, a label which allows for the presence of a variety of energies and beings that we may not always think of as Faery. This landscape of the inner world has many layers where we may encounter not only faery beings but ancient deities, those who have passed, and the deepest ancestors, on whose shoulders we all stand.

By whichever name we call it, this luminous land that exists within our own can be thought of as the original energetic template of our world. Contrary to the idea of the underworld as a place of punishment or desolation (as perpetuated by book-based religions), the more ancient truth is that it is a timeless, vibrant place of healing and restoration. This land has strong ties to Grail lore because, in a sense, the realm itself *is* the Grail, and by seeking to connect with Faery, we are all on our own Grail quest to renew our sadly damaged connection to truth and wholeness.

Vision of the Grail Hallows

Find a place where you can sit comfortably and know you will not be disturbed. Have a notebook and pen nearby in case you wish to make notes afterwards. You may find it helpful to burn some frankincense or other incense in order to aid in transporting your senses. If possible, identify which direction is east, and sit facing that direction. Once you are comfortable and settled, close your eyes and take three deep breaths in and out. Picture yourself as you are now, sitting in the room that you are in. Slowly a white mist fills your vision until you can see only white. You feel quite safe and continue to breathe steadily. The white mist soon starts to clear, revealing the interior of a small stone chapel. It is square, and you are sitting in the centre, with four short paths radiating from your position, as if you are at a crossroads. These four paths lead to nearby cube-shaped altars, one in each direction. Above each altar is a window, each of which seems to be letting in light and air from its own source.

You are facing the eastern altar, on which you see a sword. Stand and walk the path that leads to this altar, where you are bathed in dawn light from the window and a cool, refreshing breeze. As you stand before the altar, you can see the sword in more detail. You feel moved to touch the sword, and as you do so, before you a bright landscape appears over which the sun is just starting to rise. There are standing stones on a grassy plain, and within them the glimmer of something that may be a sword. You hear the name Gorias. You may stay with this moment as long as you wish and allow further impressions to come to you as they will. When you are ready to return to the chapel, release the sword and see the walls of the chapel reappear. Return to the centre.

You now turn to face the southern wall of the chapel and walk towards the altar there. The light flooding through this window is the searing gold of noon and the air is warm. On the altar in front of you is a spear. You feel moved to touch the spear, and as you do so, a wooded landscape appears before you, bathed in warm sunlight, and the name Finias appears in your mind. You instinctively know this is a glimpse of the home of the spear hallow. You may linger for further impressions and return to the chapel when you are ready.

Once again, return to the centre. Now turn to face the western wall of the chapel. As you move towards the altar, you see a silver chalice catching the amber light of the setting sun; the scent of autumn is in the air. Touch the chalice and find yourself looking out towards the ocean as the sun slowly sinks below the horizon. The name Murias is whispered on the air, and you feel there are secrets of the grail hallow to be found here. When you are ready, return to the centre of the chapel.

Turn to face north. The path leads to an altar that looks silver under the moonlight, and though there is a chill in the air, you are comfortable. On the altar lies a green palm-sized circular stone with an equal-armed cross marked on it. As you touch this stone, you find yourself in a cave deep in the earth, lit by a green light that seems to emanate from the walls themselves. You hear the name Falias and feel that there are mysteries to be learned of the stone hallow here. When you are ready, return to the stone chapel.

For a few moments, you sit back in your original position in the centre of the chapel and process what you have learned. You know that you may return as often as you wish. When you are ready to leave, the white mist reappears and fills your vision. The white mist clears, and you are back in your own reality. You may open your eyes when you are ready, take some deep breaths, and make any notes or sketches that you wish. Drink some water, have a bite to eat, and ground yourself.

The Maidens of the Wells (France)

Known as *The Elucidation*, this story by an unknown author from thirteenth-century France was written as a prologue to Chrétien de Troyes's *Perceval ou le Conte de Graal*, providing the backstory to the Grail quest and also much insight and wisdom into humanity's past relationship with Faery. It remains relevant to our world today, as it seems the lesson of how to live in harmony with the environment has not yet been learned and we are in danger of the whole planet becoming a wasteland if we do not find a way to restore the balance…

Centuries ago, in a land that was then known as Logres, abundance blessed the land. All manner of wealth and earthly delights poured forth from the kingdom of the Fisher King, and both plant and animal life thrived in all places. At this time humanity still remembered how to live in balance with the land. At this time Faery was not so far from us as it is now. During this time of plenty, there was no need of want, for whenever there was a need, it was met. Humankind only took what it needed and served the land well in return. All things were kept in balance and reciprocity. Nature and Faery respected that and always blessed requests with abundance. The source for such vibrant health in the land was the sacred water that sprang from wells tended by faery women known as the Voices of the Wells. They each had a golden chalice, a reflection of the Grail itself, from which they would pour forth water to those who requested it respectfully and provide food to any who needed it, and so the land thrived in mutual service and understanding.

So it was until a corrupt king, Amangons, and his knights came to the land. He sought the riches of the Grail for himself, without any understanding of the wisdom that accompanied it. He took without asking, and he and his knights lewdly violated the well maidens. They tried to steal the maidens' golden chalices, but such purity could

● ● ●

not be sustained in their vile grasp, and both maidens and chalices vanished from the land. The kingdom of the Grail and the Fisher King was lost, and the landscape was rendered barren and without life until such a time as the lessons could be learned and the ancient hurt between the realms healed once more.

How beautiful they are,
The lordly ones
Who dwell in the hills,
In the hollow hills.
They have faces like flowers
And their breath is wind
That blows over grass
Filled with dewy clover…

Fiona Macleod (William Sharp),
The Immortal Hour

A History of Human–Faery Relations

The path of Faery has run parallel to ours throughout time, with cultures all around the world telling tales of invisible folk who live within the land. Sightings are rare, but their presence is often felt in the wild places and in our hearts. Often the relationship between human and faery races has not been an easy one. Shifts in beliefs over the ages have meant that beings once revered and respected became feared for mischief and misdeeds. The popular modern image of faeries as diminutive winged beings may be somewhat removed from their origins and true power, but it still provides a gateway for many to connect to these guardians of nature. In our current materialistic age, some choose to mock belief in unseen forces, yet faeries and humans need each other now more than ever, and many still hear their call. But what is Faery? How can we trace the light of truth through the myths?

The History of the Sidhe

It was from the north they came; and in the place they came from had four cities, where they fought their battle for learning: great Falias, and shining Gorias, and Finias and rich Murias that lay to the south (Gregory 2006, 27).

Western Faery tradition has its roots in the ancient Irish myths of the Tuatha de Danann (children of the goddess Danu), whose descendants became known as the Aos Sí, or Daoine Sídhe. Modern mystics tend to use "Sidhe," as popularised by W. B. Yeats and others. The Book of Invasions tells us they arrived in great ships from four mysterious cities, bearing mystical objects that resonate with the four Grail hallows of Arthurian lore. From Falias came the Stone of Fal, which would let out a shout when the true king of Ireland set foot upon it. The Spear of Lugh came from the city of Gorias and granted powers of invincibility to its bearer. From Finias came the shining Sword of Nuada, which always found its target, and from Murias, the Cauldron of the Dagda, which satisfied all who fed from it.

The Tuatha de Danann were the pre-Christian gods of Ireland, radiant beings who were preceded by a race of giants known as the Firbolg. In this sense they are reminiscent of the Olympian gods replacing the Titans of Greek mythology, and this theme of an ancient race of giants that existed pre-humanity can be found in numerous cultures around the world. When an ancient race is defeated or replaced, they retreat into the earth, where their power becomes part of the inner landscape; thus, they are an important part of faery lore.

As the Tuatha de Danann in turn retreated from the world of men, they became invisible, as though they had shifted to a different frequency of existence whilst inhabiting the same space. As they faded in prominence, many of them also became known as the Sidhe, which is also the name given to the ancient burial mounds of

Ireland (or in Scotland, the Sidh/Sith). Some are still known as named faery queens and kings and as goddesses and gods within the Celtic Pagan pantheon. One of the most prominent of these is the Morrigan, goddess of warriors and battles, who survived into the Arthurian mythos as Morgan le Fay. She challenges heroes in order to strengthen them and can take on the appearance of crows. We also still remember the solar deity Lugh, from whom we have the name of the Irish harvest festival Lughnasadh, and the sea god Manannán mac Lir.

Many people have heard of the dread spirit of folklore called the banshee, whose eldritch screech may be heard when a family member is soon to die. The name banshee originates in the *bean-sidhe*, which simply means "faery woman," and it is said only certain Irish families have such ancestral spirits attending them.

In modern faery practice, the Sidhe are powerful guardians of the inner landscape who may be contacted through various means, including meditation and journeying using symbols such as the Great Glyph of the Sidhe, which we will look at later in this book. They are powerful allies who wish to work with us to restore balance to the world.

Fallen Angels

A number of cultures around the world have a similar origin myth for the faery race (or the equivalent for that country), which is that they fell from heaven and—not wishing to follow the other fallen angels into hell—settled in the hollow places of the earth. On a surface level, this may be dismissed as an attempt by the Christian monks responsible for much of the writing of historical records to demonise residing Pagan beliefs, but it is important to remember that the same myth endures in Muslim doctrine, and there are deeper truths to be found within this myth.

Angels are representatives of cosmic energy that exists within the celestial realm and radiates outward towards the earth, and faery beings are carriers of cosmic energy within the earth that radiates outward. This is a cycle of energetic transmission from the universe into our world and back again, which carries the energy of the cosmos and our souls, the life-giving, animating force that connects all things. In this sense we can see faery beings as being aspects of the anima mundi, or world soul, an important concept that we will come back to.

The Tylwyth Teg

The Welsh name for the faery folk is Tylwyth Teg, "fair family," a race of tall and fair people with a penchant for kidnapping fair-haired human children and leaving changelings in their place, hence their other, euphemistic name Bendith y Mamau, or "mother's blessing." They're reputed to live in caves, mountains, or underwater, be fond of dancing, and essentially share traits with other European, Celtic, and British faeries.

Welsh faery lore is particularly known for its faery brides, magical women who emerge from lakes and are married by mortal men but who must return to their home realm after a promise is broken. The most famous version of this, which is seen through a few tales, is that the mortal husband promises he will not strike her, even in jest, or on the third strike she must leave. Inevitably, through mishap, this occurs. It is an important lesson in being vigilant about keeping promises to our faery allies!

Arthurian Myth

The great body of works that tell the tale of the mythical King Arthur and his knights spans from the Welsh Mabinogion through Geoffrey of Monmouth's famous *History of the Kings of Britain* and Mallory's *Le Morte d'Arthur* to the French chivalric tradition. The earliest written sources, such as the Mabinogion, are taken from much older oral traditions, and though there are many theories as to whether or not Arthur himself was a real historical figure, the tales are derived from old Celtic legends of gods, heroes, and faeries.

As previously mentioned, Morgan le Fay is an important figure in these tales, with various manifestations and variations occurring through the ages. As the Welsh Morgen she is one of nine priestesses with powers of healing and prophecy. Later she becomes Arthur's half sister and also chief foe, yet she is also one of the queens who accompanies him in his final hours to the sacred Isle of Avalon. When reading the legends, the roles of some female characters in particular may appear morally ambiguous and confusing; it is important to remember that usually the stories passed from oral tradition into writing via Christian monks, who would of course put their own spin on events.

In some later versions, Morgan becomes conflated with fellow faery woman Nimue as lover and eventual rival to Merlin, but Nimue is an important figure in her own right. There are some layers of misogynistic and anti-Pagan propaganda that must be scraped away to reach the truth, but as Lady of the Lake and keeper of the otherworld gates, Nimue is a powerful ally and teacher. Does she trap Merlin in the underworld or is she his priestess-lover, the keeper of the door that allows him to rest there and be renewed? It is Nimue who bestows Excalibur upon Arthur, a sign that the guardians of the inner world support his rulership. The Lady of the Lake and the Celtic goddesses from which she is descended are representations of sovereignty, and by working with them today we may learn to wield our own power responsibly.

Nimue Meditation Journey

Sit comfortably in a place where you will not be disturbed. You may wish to have a notebook and pen handy to write down your experience afterwards. Take three deep breaths, and with each breath out, relax your body and mind further, releasing the tensions of the day. As you breathe out for a third time, gently close your eyes and visualise yourself sitting in the room, just as you are. See a white mist start to appear. It feels safe and welcoming as it fills your vision until all you can see is white. As the mist starts to dissipate, a new scene forms.

You are standing in the clearing of a forest on a moonlit night. The sky is perfectly clear and the moon is full. Before you is a tranquil lake, mirroring perfectly the sky above. The reflection of the moon seems to form a silver path on the water, and you step forward into it, knowing that all is well. As you step into the water, the silver path forms descending stairs, which you follow down beneath the lake. You find that you can breathe easily.

.

As you reach the bottom of the silver stairs, you see a beautiful palace before you that appears to be made of glass. The gate is open, and you feel the urge to enter. As you pass through the gate into a long hallway, silver light glistens all around you and you hear gentle music that sounds like bells and chimes. Lining the corridor are many statues of figures from different eras of history. Somehow they feel familiar to you. You notice a raised dais at the end of a hall with an empty throne upon it. A figure stands next to it, beckoning you to approach.

As you reach the figure, you see it is an ethereal woman clad in shimmering silver who seems to be awaiting a question.

You ask, "Who sits in the throne?"

In a deep and melodic voice, she replies, "It has not yet been claimed. It is the seat of your own power. Will you claim it?"

If you choose to, you may now step forward and take your place in the glass throne, which feels as though it has been waiting for you.

The lady speaks:

"This is the secret that humankind has lost: that each of you is ruler of yourselves. You and the land are one, and all people are as one within the land. Hold this key close to your heart so that others may not sway you from your path, and use your power wisely."

She hands you an object or symbol. Thank her and be sure to remember this object well as it is a source of personal power to you. She speaks to you once more.

"Return now to your realm above, and remember well this place and what you have learned. Know that you may return whenever you need restoration and that your inner self is now enthroned in power."

You bid farewell to the lady, keeping her gift to you safe. As you walk back down the hall, you realise that the statues you pass are your own ancestors, tracing your lineage back through the centuries. You ascend the stairs and emerge from the lake onto the shore as the first golden rays of dawn are starting to appear. How long were you below the surface? As you contemplate this question, the white mist reappears and fills your vision once more. When it dissipates you see yourself back in the room. With three deep breaths, open your eyes and make notes of your experience. You may wish to find or create a physical representation of the symbol or object you were gifted as a focus for personal power in your daily life.

Thomas the Rhymer

He has gotten a coat of the even cloth,
And a pair of shoes of velvet green,
And, till seven years were gane and past,
True Thomas on earth was never seen.

Sir Walter Scott, "Thomas the Rhymer"

The ballad "Thomas the Rhymer" tells the seemingly fantastical tale of a man who is taken into Faery by the queen of the faeries and becomes her lover for seven years, and upon his return to mortal realms is gifted with the tongue that cannot lie—the gift of prophecy. Though there are various versions of his tale in literature that survive, going back to the fifteenth century, Thomas was, in fact, a real historical figure who wrote many prophetic verses during his life in the thirteenth century, earning him a reputation to rival Merlin himself.

Irish Folklore

Most of what we now think of as faery lore is derived from primarily Irish folklore, which was a mostly oral tradition. Such terms as "the little people" or "good neighbours" were not meant to literally describe faeries but to make them less fearful when spoken about. It was of utmost importance to keep in good favour with any local faery beings, with regular offerings being made and great care taken not to build on the faery roads, or paths through the landscape that faeries used. Ill fortune would befall anyone foolish or ignorant enough to defy them, and these beliefs survive to this day, with a number of contemporary news stories featuring people who have suffered bad fortune after either building on a faery road or moving part of the landscape considered sacred to the "good people." Stories are passed down through the generations, and many of these were recorded by folklorists such as Lady Gregory and Walter Evans-Wentz in their fascinating works *Visions and Beliefs in the West of Ireland* (1920) and *The Fairy-Faith in Celtic Countries* (1911), respectively.

Shakespeare

O, then I see Queen Mab hath been with you…
She is the fairies' midwife and she comes,
In shape no bigger than an agate stone,
On the forefinger of an alderman…

. . . .

Shakespeare, *Romeo and Juliet*

Faeries' shift in image in popular culture from dark and powerful to the delicate and diminutive flower fairy can be traced back to the works of Shakespeare, though it seems unlikely that this would have been his intention. In A *Midsummer Night's Dream*, we are presented with an extremely potent queen and king of Faery, Titania and Oberon, whose quarreling affects the very balance of nature itself. We are also introduced to the mischievous Puck, inspired by the hobgoblins and pooka of British folklore, given his first known appearance in literature by Shakespeare. However, there are also Titania's faeries, with names such as Mustardseed and Peaseblossom, who are able to make themselves small enough to hide in acorn cups. *Romeo and Juliet* also brings us a vision of tiny faeries in the famous Queen Mab speech delivered by the romantically jaded Mercutio.

The popularity of these plays and such a romantic and nonthreatening version of Faery had a big influence on audiences and writers of the time. In the Elizabethan era, belief in faeries was still the norm, and the romantic chivalric faery mythology was perpetuated by works such as Spenser's *Faerie Queene*, which equated Queen Elizabeth with the queen of Faery. However, with Elizabeth's passing, magical belief started to wane in the rise of humanist philosophy and was condemned during the Jacobean era in the dawn of the seventeenth century, and the popular entertainment of the time echoed this shift. Unlike his contemporaries, who made light of magical beliefs or showed them to be damnable folly in their works, Shakespeare filled his last plays with occult imagery and supernatural beings, with his final play, *The Tempest*, being the most magical of all.

. . . .

Ye elves of hills, brooks, standing lakes and groves,
And ye that on the sands with printless foot
Do chase the ebbing Neptune and do fly him
When he comes back...

Reverend Kirk and the Secret Commonwealth

> These *siths*, or fairies, they call *Sleigh Maith*, or the Good People, it
> would seem, to prevent the dint of their ill attempts (for the Irish
> use to bless all they fear harm of) and are said to be of a middle
> nature betwixt man and angel, as were daemons thought to be of
> old; of intelligent studious spirits, and light changeable bodies
> (like those called astral) somewhat of the nature of a condensed
> cloud, and best seen in twilight.

One of the most remarkable pieces of folkloric writing comes
from an author who became folklore himself, the Reverend Robert Kirk, who wrote the above in his book *The Secret Commonwealth*.
He was born in 1644 in Aberfoyle, in the wild Scottish Highlands,
where his father was a minister. After graduating from Edinburgh
University in 1661, he served in the parish of Balquidder, where he
married Isobel Campbell and had one son, Colin. After Isobel's death
in 1680, he returned to Aberfoyle and took up his father's old post,
abiding near the famous Faery Hill. It is thought that many of his
extraordinary observations of the nature of faery beings were based
on his own experiences of them, and when he was found lifeless at
the top of Faery Hill in 1692, many believe that his spirit was taken
into Faery. Indeed, many who travel between the realms have met

him in the otherworld acting as an envoy, a psychopomp between our world and theirs.

The Victorians

Depictions of faery in popular art reached a peak in the Victorian era, built on a foundation laid in the preceding decades by visionary artists such as William Blake and eighteenth-century fantasy artist Henry Fuseli. One of the most exceptional faery artists of the Victorian era is Richard Dadd, who is sadly best remembered for spending the majority of his life in mental institutions but who painted images based on both literary works and his own visions of Faery. The Scottish artist Joseph Noel Paton also painted images of Faery, again inspired by the works of Shakespeare, and the Pre-Raphaelite Brotherhood created many beautiful visions of Faery, taking inspiration from literature, myth, and poetry.

The Victorians were fascinated by Faery and the spirit world, and this era saw a surge in folkloric writing and visionary poetry as well as the visual arts. Another notable artist whose work continued to bring the enchantment of Faery into the world is the illustrator Arthur Rackham, who captured the fluidity and vibrancy of Faery with his pen-and-ink drawings.

Faery in the Twentieth Century

The enthusiasm for all things Faery continued into the early twentieth century, with many visionary writers and artists keen to explore the hidden realms and create works inspired by ancient lore. W. B. Yeats and Lady Gregory were two of the most significant figures to emerge in the Irish literary scene, whose legacy endures to this day. Yeats was keen to explore the mystery traditions, including becoming a member of the esoteric order called the Golden Dawn, and this influence may be seen in his poems and plays. He accompanied Lady Gregory for some of her travels around Ireland collecting the valuable accounts of faery encounters and other folklore, which were published as *Visions and Beliefs in the West of Ireland* (1920).

J. M. Barrie's *Peter Pan* added to the literary representation of faery, bringing us one of the most iconic portrayals in the mischievous and often morally ambiguous Tinker Bell. Sir Arthur Conan Doyle, best known for creating the ultimate logical detective, Sherlock Holmes, was also fascinated by the world of Faery and was so convinced that the Cottingley fairies were real that he wrote *The Coming of the Fairies* in 1922.

The Cottingley Fairies

In 1917 cousins Elsie Wright and Frances Griffiths of Cottingley, West Yorkshire, took a series of photographs with Elsie's father's camera in an attempt to prove that their stories about why they were spending time playing down by the "beck" (a stream in a forest) were true. Many believed the photos of the fairies they claimed to see were real, right up until the 1980s. They can't have possibly expected at the time that the photos would have ended up in the hands of the Theosophical Society, causing such a sensation throughout society.

Many, including Sir Arthur Conan Doyle, were convinced the photos were genuine, despite them being quite obviously cardboard cut outs, a fact that the women eventually confessed to in their old age. It was a bleak time for all after the First World War, and people were desperately wanting to believe in a world beyond. Perhaps it was the earnest nature of the children that convinced people. After all, they maintained that although they had staged the photographs, they had seen faeries on many occasions and had only made the photos in an attempt to prove what they had experienced to skeptical adults.

Flower Fairies

When many people think of faeries, the image that comes to mind is that of Cicely Mary Barker's flower fairies. These charming illustrations show botanically accurate flowers, each with their own "fairy," which were portraits of small children dressed to match the plants and accompanied by short verses. Her first book of illustrations was Flower Fairies of the Spring, published in 1923, followed by books for fairies of summer, autumn, and many more during her lifetime.

Barker died in 1973, and Flower Fairies of Winter was published posthumously in 1985, followed by many more, with her images becoming part of popular culture. Although it is not an accurate portrayal of Faery, her work does encourage good plant folklore knowledge and an animistic perspective that can be useful when working with nature spirits.

Findhorn

It is important for the future of mankind that
belief in the Nature Spirits and their god Pan
is re-established and that they are seen in
their true light and not misunderstood.

. . . .

Paul Hawken, *The Magic of Findhorn*

In 1962 three spiritually attuned people were led to a remote location in the far northeast of Scotland, where they laid the foundations for what was to become the extraordinary community of Findhorn. Beginning with the seeds of necessity (a lack of money meaning they needed to grow vegetables in sandy soil), they used their spiritual gifts to communicate with the spirits of nature, beginning a lifelong collaboration with extraordinary results. By communicating with the spirits of place and plants, they were able to grow not only vegetables but a thriving garden. Over time Findhorn grew to become an artistic and spiritual community where all work in harmony with their surroundings and the spirits within the landscape. The 1980s saw the beginnings of an eco-village to house members of the community with minimal environmental impact, and at the time of writing these number ninety! Findhorn has gone from strength to strength, a beacon of hope in a challenging age.

The Fairy Flag of Dunvegan

On the magical Isle of Skye, a small island off the west coast of Scotland, is Castle Dunvegan, the ancestral home of the clan Macleod. One of their most treasured artifacts is a banner that, legend has it, was gifted to the chief of the clan many centuries ago by the faeries. In some versions of the tale, it was a gift from a faery queen who was his lover. She charmed it with the power to grant victory to the clan in battle, but it could only be called on three times. The chief used the banner to secure victory for his clan twice, but as far as lore has it, the third charm is still intact. The now very fragile banner is kept framed and on display at Dunvegan Castle, and though belief in Faery may not be as widespread as it was, many still believe in the potency of the flag and that one day it will bring glory to the clan Macleod once again.

Faery Festivals

Belief in Faery has been enjoying a strong revival in recent years, with many festivals being organised around the globe, attended by hundreds of people all year round. Though on the surface these events may look like an escapist excuse to dress up and forget about the troubling times we live in, it is a way for those who share a connection and love for Faery to gather and celebrate together. In most cases it is a belief that working with Faery can help us to make the world a better place which drives these gatherings, and there are also often workshops and lectures as well as parties and fun. The resurgence in Faery belief and practice has forged a strong community around the world that transcends political and geographic boundaries and unites the hearts of many.

Faeries in Pop Culture

Although the peak of Faery prevalence in pop culture was in the art, theatre, and poetry of the Victorian era, there has been a revival of interest and representation of faery beings in the popular entertainment of our modern and postmodern age, with many movies from the 1980s featuring fantastic creatures and tales. *Legend* starred a young Tom Cruise and a beast-like Tim Curry in a beautiful fairy-tale, *Willow* imagined a quest for freedom in a land oppressed by dark magic, and *Labyrinth* brought us the legendary David Bowie as the Goblin King in a world imagined by the combined genius of Jim Henson and artist Brian Froud.

More recent imaginings have taken a darker turn. *Pan's Labyrinth* and *Hellboy* II both bring Guillermo del Toro's extraordinary vision of Faery to the screen in a very powerful way that is not for children or the faint of heart, and recently the Amazon Original series *Carnival Row* has taken a film noir approach to the subject.

However, movies such as *Maleficent* feel like a return to the feel of the fantasy films of the 80s. It seems that in times when materialism threatens to swallow us whole, we reach out in our hearts for magic and wonder. While we still do this, there is hope.

UFOs

There is a notable amount of crossover between the modern folklore phenomenon of unidentified flying objects, alien kidnappings, and faery lore. The classic types of aliens that are described fit with descriptions of faery beings from folklore and contemporary mystical experience, even including large, hairy beings, which fit descriptions of hobgoblins and faery beings from the more rugged parts of Scotland. They share the phenomenon of lost time, are both blamed for crop circles, and the more esoteric amongst UFO aficionados maintain that they come from deep within the earth, just like faery beings.

Those who wish to believe we have been visited by aliens may say that this means faery visitations in folklore were actually aliens all along. Although I do believe there must be alien life out there—simple maths and probability, apart from anything else—and don't discount the chance that they may have visited us at some point, knowing that faery beings appear to us in forms affected by our own psychological filters, I tend to believe it's the other way around: that with the advent of space travel and new technology, it is easier for the human mind to experience aliens than accept faeries, so that is what they perceive. When they encounter the faery energies of inner earth, their brain interprets it as something extraterrestrial. Perhaps the truth is a mixture of both—another reflection of the interconnectedness of all things.

Faeries Around the World

Whilst the folklore of what we know as faery is primarily British, European, and Celtic in origin, if we go beyond the known labels, we can find similar beings in many cultures around the world, with natures that reflect the landscape and culture they originate from. The name "faery" comes from the Latin word *fata*, meaning otherworldly women who represented the forces of Fate.

In the Nordic myths, not only are there women known as the Norns, a race of beings who weave the fates of humankind, but also the *Alfar* and *Svartalfar*, or elves and dark elves, as well as ice giants and other mythical beings that all would fit under the umbrella term of what we now understand as "faery." Iceland in particular has a strong belief in the importance and power of faery beings, whom they know as *Huldufólk* (Hidden People)—invisible beings who live in certain rocks. Consideration is still given to these sacred places when planning construction.

Russia also has its fair share of faery beings, including domestic spirits called *domovoi* who could be encouraged with offerings to help with protecting the household and would sometimes accompany families when they moved to a different house.

It is not only cooler climes that have their faeries. The djinn of Arabian and Islamic culture bear many similarities to the faery beings of ancient Celtic tradition, the word *djinn* or *jinn* meaning "hidden," and they are also described as being between human and angel nature. The Westernised version of these beings will be more familiar to you as genies, and the popular story of Aladdin is from a Middle Eastern tale of the powers of the djinn. A West African culture has their equivalent in the benevolent spirits of nature known as the Aziza. In Hindu beliefs the spiritual guardians of the natural world are known as Vidyeshvaras, and Greek mythology is rife with the saucy antics of nymphs, dryads, and satyrs.

Native American culture has a profound respect for spirits of all kinds and an animistic belief that all things in nature are possessed of spirits that can be communicated with. Faery beings in Native American culture are given different names by different tribes, of course, but their essence remains the same.

Another fascinating aspect of faery belief around the globe is how certain beings seem to travel with the people of the region they have come from; for example, leprechauns have been seen by some on the streets of America in areas with a high level of Irish immigration. As with all these facts, here there are layers of truth and belief to investigate that can lead to deeper wisdom.

Why Work with Faery?

Now that we have learned some of the history and lore about our faery cousins, why should we work with them? We cannot divide our relationship with faery from our relationship with the natural world, and just as humanity's treatment of the environment has been less than ideal (to put it mildly), so has our relationship with faery. Of the three ancestral threads that weave our world together—human, animal, and faery—humanity has been too selfishly focused on our own interests at the expense of the others, and the majority have shifted away from believing in anything beyond their immediately tangible world.

For those of us who feel the call to do so, who are open to awareness of the inner worlds and who hear the song in our hearts, it is more important than ever to build the strong connection needed to help restore balance to a world that is rapidly descending into chaos. We must follow the call and find the hidden roads that lead to Faery. If you are ready, let's move on to the next chapter and look at the different gateways that we may journey through together…

Bran and the Silver Bough (Ireland)

Apple trees are very important in faery lore as a symbol of the wisdom of the otherworld, and silver or golden apple branches may be found in a number of myths and tales from Celtic and Greek lore. They act as a sort of passport to the otherworld, and it is still an emblem of key importance to some modern Pagan paths with a Celtic influence, especially symbolising the poetic and musical inspiration that comes from the otherworld. This story, which is a traditional tale from approximately eighth-century Ireland, also deals with the themes of faery queens as initiators and lost time when taken into Faery...

. . .

In the age of myth and heroes, when men were closer to the gods and faery folk walked freely in the world, there lived a high king whose name was Bran. Bran was a good and wise king, but he grew weary of the call of responsibility and the constant noise of court, and one evening he left yet another tedious feast to seek out a place where he could find peace and solitude.

Walking alone through the forest, the sounds of the feast left far behind him, Bran started to hear an enchanting music, the likes of which he had never before heard. When he tried to follow the sound, however, it eluded him, as whichever way he turned, it seemed to always be coming from right behind him. Regardless of this frustration, the ethereal music brought great peace to his otherwise troubled mind, and eventually he settled down to rest.

Eyes closed in slumber, the king dreamt of a beautiful otherworldly woman who sang to his soul. She sang of a place called the Island of Women, where he could find true peace. There, there was no conflict, no grief, no infernal politics to contend with; simply love and harmony. When he awoke, he found he was holding a silver branch with golden apples on it. He had no idea where it had come from, but refreshed by his dream, he returned to his castle, taking the branch with him.

The next night at the feast, the woman from his dream appeared again, but this time he was awake, and everyone at the feast could see her! He still was holding the silver branch, and when she told him once more of the Island of Women and gave him directions of where to find her there, the branch left his hand and flew to her, at which point she vanished.

Full of fire from his visions, Bran immediately set out to build a ship and put a crew together for his journey to find the Island of Women. He took with him his three foster brothers, and they in turn took nine of their men, and they sailed far to the west, beyond the known boundaries of men.

On their voyage they encountered many wonders. The god of the sea, Manannán mac Lir, rose up beside them on his chariot to tell them they were in fields of flowers, not on waves and sea foam, and described his magical kingdom under the sea. They then came across land; it was not the Island of Women but the Island of Joy. When they shouted their questions of where to find the Island of Women to those on the shore, they only laughed at them, seemingly out of their senses. One of Bran's crew left the ship to question them further, but he himself became lost to the mindless mirth of the natives of the island. Fearing they would come to the same fate, Bran and his remaining crew left him to his endless laughter and continued on their quest.

When they did eventually find the Island of Women, which they knew as they recognised the woman from Bran's vision and the feast standing on the shore, they were cautious of landing ashore because of what had happened to their crew member on the Island of Joy, but the woman cast out a thread to draw them in, and that night they all feasted in a great palace. The feast was magnificent, with plates and cups that would renew with every bite or sip and never empty. The palace was full of beautiful and intelligent women who cared for each member of the crew, and at the end of the day, they were all taken to chambers to sleep with the women.

They stayed with the enchanting women for what seemed to be a year, and all that time were at peace, but one of the men grew restless and wished to return home. Eventually Bran agreed, but the woman warned him that returning would only bring grief. When he insisted they must return home, she made him promise that he would not set foot on the shore.

So, Bran and his crew set off on their voyage home to Ireland, rescuing their lost crewman from the Island of Joy on the way. However, when they approached their old home, they found it changed.

● ● ●

What had once been a land rich and green with forests was transformed, and even its people seemed diminished. All was dull and
grey, and a feeling of dread fell upon them. They called out to people
on the shore, but they had never heard of them until an old man told
them he remembered stories about a king called Bran being told to
him when he was a child, but it was a myth from long ago. Bran realised that while they had been with the women for what seemed like
only a year, they had, in fact, been absent for many centuries.

His crewman who had so missed home refused to accept that
the world he knew was gone and leapt overboard to swim to shore,
where he turned to dust.

Realising they could never return home, Bran and his crew set
sail once more, never to be seen in this world again. Perhaps they are
sailing still...

The lady sayd, re we climb yon hill,
And I will show you fairlies three...

Sir Walter Scott, "Thomas the Rhymer"

The Road
to Faery

The world of Faery exists alongside, beneath, and within the world as we perceive it; therefore, once we acknowledge the truth of its existence, it makes sense that there are many points of intersection between their world and ours. Equally, just as each of us perceives and processes the world in different ways, different methods of accessing the otherworld work better for different people. The exercises that we've already worked on in this book are all designed to help build your ability to connect and sense beyond the material realm. We will now look at taking further steps on the road to Faery and making all-important allies along the way.

Imagination as a Tool

I'm sure we've all heard "but that's all imaginary" or "it's just in your head," and equally anyone who has walked a spiritual or magical path will sensibly check themselves at times as to whether experiences are real or imaginary. In a world that does not always prioritise creativity and magic, it's easy to dismiss imagination as meaningless, but our imagination can be trained to become one of the most powerful tools at our disposal.

As we have already discussed, perceiving energetic beings that exist on a different frequency or vibration to what we are accustomed can be tricky. Our minds must find a way to interpret the information by drawing upon things within our experience. If we expand our experience through visualisation exercises and continue to open our hearts and other empathic receptors, our imagination—our ability to visualise what is not physically in front of us—gains a wider palette of colours and detail that it can use to interpret energetic and empathic impressions into a clearer and more accurate signal. Once we have practiced visualisations such as the ones in this book and have them to the point where we can see the described details clearly, as well as new details that also come through and feel authentic, then we are ready to trust our otherworldly perceptions with more freedom in some of the following techniques.

Entering an Image

Do you have a favourite faery artist? Is there a particular image or set of images that resonates with you, that stirs something in your soul? Perhaps you already have a tarot or oracle deck you could use, or—if all these ideas are new to you—why not have a search for a piece of artwork that depicts an otherwordly landscape or being?

If you're not sure where to start, search for images by Brian Froud, Charles Vess, Arthur Rackham, Marc Potts, Linda Ravenscroft, and Julia Jeffrey (or, indeed, do take a look at my own artwork for *Tarot of the Sidhe*). It is best to begin with an image that has a distinct landscape you feel you could step into, rather than just a figure or portrait. Equally, you may wish to try this with a photograph of a sacred site that has connections to Faery. We will talk more about crossover points in the landscape in the next chapter.

Entering an Image

Find a place where you can sit comfortably and uninterrupted, with your chosen image before you. Also have a notebook and pen handy for afterwards. Either holding the image in your hands or with it resting on a surface near you, spend time really taking in every detail of the image. Experiment with closing your eyes and seeing if you can re-create it in your vision, then opening your eyes again and work on filling in any gaps. Now start engaging the other imaginative sense in this process. Is there a breeze? Are there any scents on the air? Is it warm or cold? What noises would you be able to hear if you stood within the image? How would it move? When you are satisfied that you have build a complete mental image, and you can see and feel the picture before you in its entirety with your eyes closed, close your eyes.

Now, seeing the landscape from your image before you, take a step forward into the image. Is it light or dark? How does the air feel? Can you reach out and touch any part of the landscape before you? (Don't touch any beings without permission!) Can you hear anything? Smell anything? Allow the landscape to become alive before you.

If there are any beings present, introduce yourself politely and make it clear that your intents are honourable. They may respond. Give this moment the time and space needed to develop naturally. Do they give you anything to take back to your world? Do you have anything you can leave with them in return or is there anything else you wish to say to each other? If there is no being present in your image at first, see whether one may appear or even if you sense one, as they may not be visible.

When your experience in this landscape comes to a natural end, bid farewell to any beings you have met and step back out of the image into your own reality once more. Open your eyes when you are ready, ground yourself, and make notes to help you remember details.

You may repeat this exercise as often as you wish, either with the same image or different images, and it will likely become more vivid as you gain experience.

Journeying Using a Symbol

Symbols, sigils, and glyphs have a number of magical uses, such as invocation, evocation, empowering objects, healing, and as a focus for magical intent. They have also long been used in meditation, and they can make effective gateways to other realms, such as Faery. Indeed, it is possible that you may be given symbols in your dreams or meditations once you start this work, so be sure to always make a quick sketch so that they're not forgotten! When you are given a symbol in a meditation, try to remember to ask what its purpose is. Though the answer you get may not always be clear, you may get a good sense of how you can use it.

The Great Glyph of the Sidhe

One symbol that is particularly effective as a gateway is the Great Glyph of the Sidhe (see page 94). This labyrinthian symbol (some have compared it to Cho Ku Rei, the Reiki healing symbol) was discovered by author and mystic John Matthews in the early 2000s. He immediately started to introduce it to his students in workshops and to the world at large in his book *The Sidhe: Wisdom of the Celtic Otherworld* (Lorian, 2004). It provides a direct link to their realm; when incorporated into artwork, it aids in creating art that bridges the worlds. Experiences vary, but it is safe to use, and a common agreement is that using the glyph helps bring our worlds closer together.

EXERCISE

Great Glyph of the Sidhe Meditation

Copy the symbol on the facing page onto a larger piece of paper, card, canvas, or other surface (I once painted it on a piece of slate for an outdoor shrine), making sure there's good contrast between the symbol and its background, dark and light If possible to do so safely, prop the image of the symbol up on a surface lit by two candles, one on either side.

Be sure that you will not be disturbed. Sit comfortably while facing the symbol. Take three deep breaths and allow tension to leave your body. Much like when you were entering an image, keep your gaze on the symbol until you can see it with your eyes closed.

Once you have reached this point, keep your eyes closed and imagine the spiral becoming a tunnel that stretches out before you. Move through the tunnel and emerge on the other side. Be open to feelings, sights, scents, and sounds. You may instantly have a vivid experience or it may take a few attempts on different occasions. Be sure to address and treat any beings you meet with respect, be they human, animal, faery, plant, or other.

When your experience comes to a natural conclusion, give thanks and return through the spiral corridor. Open your eyes when you are ready—no need to rush—and make notes of your experience.

The Underworld Journey

Once the imaginative sense has been developed and honed, it is possible to explore the otherworld with more freedom, though for safety (and sense), your first journey should be to find an otherworldy ally. Once you have an ally in place, they can help you learn more about the work you are called to do and also help you find more allies with specialised skills to help you. You should always be accompanied by an ally when you journey; they will also be on hand in your everyday life for support and guidance when you call on them. Remember, though: they are not your little helpers; it is a reciprocal relationship, and there may well be tasks that they need *your* help accomplishing in *this* world! Always be mindful and respectful of this.

Before undertaking the following journey, it is important to choose a real-life location that you have visited physically and that you can visualise strongly as your starting point. This will be your entrance to the otherworld as well as your anchor to this world, and it's best if it's somewhere you have a strong connection to. Is there a tree that you know which has a natural hole amongst its roots? A gap in a hedge? A natural well, perhaps? What's the first place that comes to mind if you imagine, Alice-like, tumbling through it into

Wonderland? Take some time to really build a strong image of this place in your head before attempting the following exercise.

It is also worth trying a shamanic drumming track to help you enter an altered state of consciousness. If you have someone who has a bodhran handy and can keep a steady beat, ideal! Listening to the waves of sound formed by the resonance of the drum, in between the beats, can really help in your journeying. Others find it intrusive and can journey perfectly well without. Some may prefer white noise, a rattle, wave sounds, or other ways of shifting the consciousness. There's no rush; take the time to find a method that works best for you.

Underworld Journey
to Find Your Ally

It is exceptionally important for this exercise that you find a space and time where you will definitely not be disturbed (fellow parents, I sympathise) You will need an average of twenty minutes in order to enter the altered state and allow time to accomplish your goal. Don't worry if it doesn't work the first time, either. Remember, you are training your mind and spirit to work together in a particular way, and that will work differently for all of us.

Either in a darkened room or with a blindfold or scarf to block out light (and begin your drumming track if you are using one—headphones are fine), lie on your back on the floor, with a blanket to keep from getting chilly if you need it. (Some have blankets which they use specifically for journey work, both to lie under and on top of, and this is a good idea if you continue onwards with this work.) Take as many deep breaths as you need to release tension. Feel daily concerns melting away into the floor.

See the location in this world that you have chosen as your entry point clearly in front of you. It may be that in this world the gap or hole that it presents would be difficult for you to fit through, but those rules no longer apply. You are able to fit through the hole and enter into darkness.

Your sight adjusts as you enter, and you find yourself at the top of a spiral stair with the roots of trees around you, dimly lit by torchlight. As you descend, take in as much detail as you can. How do the walls feel to touch? What scents are on the air? What can you hear? You continue down the stairs, spiraling down, for some time. Gradually the stairs start to brighten and open wider, and you find yourself entering a great cavern that appears to be illuminated by its own light. You notice many entrances to the cavern, with passageways beyond, and the roots of a great tree that have pushed through the earth and are growing all around you. You may see symbols on the walls or over doorways, and if so, try to remember them in order to sketch them when you return.

In front of you, sitting amongst the roots of the tree, you see a great being who appears to be part man, part beast, holding a staff. He may address you first, in which case respond truthfully and politely. If he simply awaits your approach, you may greet him with respect and state that you are there to seek an otherworldly ally to aid you in your further journeying and collaboration with the realm of Faery. If he has further questions, answer from your heart. When he is satisfied, he will beat his staff upon the ground and various beings will start to appear from the other entrances. Some may be animal, some more human in appearance, and others may resemble nothing you have encountered before. It may be that only one appears. Some may appear aggressive, others disinterested—these are not for you today. If any approach you, ask if they are to become your ally or if they have a message for you.

If you find one who communicates that they are to work with you, ask them to accompany you back to your realm. Travel back up the spiral stairs together and emerge at your starting point. If it feels right to do so, you may linger here and converse further with your newfound companion. If you are ready to return or *the drumming signals it is time to return (this is a rapid beat), then open your eyes and know you can return when you wish to take further journeys, on which your ally can assist you. They may also have suggestions for work that is to be done. Be sure to take down notes, as the details will fade rapidly. Now drink some water and have a bite to eat to ground yourself.*

Back to Nature

Alongside developing your inner world tools, it is important to keep your magical work rooted in the natural world around you, otherwise it can be dangerous to slip into that all-too-tempting (and difficult to return from) realm of illusion. Most of us, even if we live in cities, have access to nature and the four elements in some form. Most cities have parks and trees. If you are confined to a very urban environment, you can usually manage a couple of potted plants! To keep returning to the four elements as the essential building blocks of the natural world, building our understanding of and relationship with them, will help keep our connection to Faery rooted in truth.

The Four Elements

As we have already touched on, the four elements in the Western mystery tradition are earth, air, fire, and water, which correspond to the directions north, east, south, and west, respectively. There are different systems, of course, but for our purposes we will be working with this system. If you already have a different understanding that works better for your culture and location, then please feel free to adapt these simple contemplations in whatever way you wish

We have already explored the energy of the deepest and purest roots of these elements through the Grail hallows, and now let's return to their emanation in the tangible world around us. For the following contemplations, it is strongly advised to find an outdoor location where you can sit relatively undisturbed for a few minutes. If you are absolutely unable to do so, it is fine to visualise the location as described, but try to have a physical representation of the element at hand, i.e., a stone or potted plant for earth, incense (or even just a window letting in a breeze) for air, a candle for fire, and a bowl of water for water (or get in the bath/shower)! When performing these contemplations, note which of your senses gives you the strongest impression. Which sense most moves your heart? This will be the most likely way that you will first start to perceive Faery.

Contemplation of Earth

Find a peaceful location where you can sit amongst trees—even just one tree you can sit under is good. See how the tree's strength is drawn from its roots growing deep underground. If you can sit or stand with your back against its trunk, feel it supporting you. Feel the ground beneath your feet. Close your eyes. Can you smell the green earth? What sounds do you hear from the trees and any fellow creatures around you? How does it feel to touch? Consider how the earth sustains you and nourishes you and how the physical body passes into this element upon death to become part of the living world.

Now turn your awareness within. Feel the strength of your own body, of the bones and sinews that make your form, the frame that contains your spirit, the cells that make up that frame. Your physical form enables you to interact with the world. How might your own form compare to the tree's? Stay with this awareness for a moment. Consider how we are part of nature, all connected by the element of earth. Open your eyes when ready, and repeat regularly.

Contemplation of Air

Find an elevated place that is exposed to the sky where you can stand or sit uninterrupted for a few minutes. Look at the sky. Are there any clouds moving above you? Birds flying? Observe them and keep your focus purely on them for a moment, considering the forces at work. Now close your eyes. Feel the wind or breeze as it moves around you; feel it on your skin. Are there any scents on the wind? Are there any sounds made by leaves or grass that air may be moving?

Now shift your focus inward. Be aware of your breathing, the steady rhythm of in and out. Here is the element of air at work within your body. The air you breathe out becomes part of the world around you, being taken in by trees and plants, who in turn make the air you breathe. Spend some time in contemplation of how the element of air connects you to the world of nature, always. Open your eyes when ready and repeat as often as you wish, perhaps trying different weather conditions and seeing how they change your perceptions.

Contemplation of Fire

You may be inside for this contemplation, preferably by a window where you can feel the sun on your face as you sit or stand comfortably without being disturbed. Light a candle in an appropriate holder and place it in front of you. First let your awareness fall on the candle. Where does the light reach? How does the flame move? Now consider the sun shining upon you and how the light touches all things and reflects back to you. Consider how the light and shadow give depth to the world around you. Close your eyes. Can you feel the heart of the sun on your skin? Can you feel the candle? How the smaller light is like an echo of the great universal power?

Now turn your awareness within and consider all those electrical impulses that run through your body, all those signals and instructions, some conscious, many unconscious. This is the element of fire at work within your body. Now consider your energy field and your spirit—how you in turn are part of the great light of the world, how energy is sent down into the world from above and emanated outward again. This is the mystery of fire and how we are all connected by it.

Contemplation of Water

For this contemplation, try to find a peaceful outdoor location where you can be near a natural source of water: the sea, a lake, a river, or even out in the rain. Touch the water and feel its coolness. Consider how the water flows around you and all solid objects, how with time it can wear away even rock. Look at how the water glistens in the light, constantly shifting. Now close your eyes and listen to the water. Does it sound musical or rhythmic in any way? Does damp air feel different or smell differently when you breathe it in?

Now allow your awareness to shift within. Be aware of the blood flowing through your body, constantly working unconsciously within us. Feel the saliva within your mouth, the wetness and potential of tears in your eyes. The human body consists of around the same percentage of water as the surface of the planet. Be aware of how we are all connected through the element of water within ourselves and the world. Open your eyes when ready.

Shutting Down, Grounding, and Shielding

We've done a lot of work now on opening up the senses and energetic centres in order to increase awareness, sensitivity, and connection. However, it can be not only draining but dangerous to conduct your life permanently in that state, and it's important to be able to maintain boundaries and close down when you need to. The key is to be in control of your energies and your boundaries! Here are some tips for keeping yourself safe:

- If you're feeling vulnerable or you know you're going to be around people in a situation that might be draining—even just taking a trip into town—try visualising a sphere or egg of light around yourself. Imagine you're a spaceship raising its shields or a knight donning armour—whatever works best for you.

- If visualising is difficult for you, then choose an object you can carry on your person or wear—a pendant or other piece of jewelery is ideal—that you can charge with protective energy and make a simple ritual of putting on and taking off. You *know* when you are out with it on that you are protected. If it is a symbol or stone that has protective qualities, even better.

- Once you have established contact with your faery ally in the underworld journey, you can meet them again and ask them to show you a symbol you can use for protection. You can then visualise this symbol in your energy field and/or draw it onto an object or paper to carry with you.

- Always be sure to ground after doing any energy work or spiritual practice. For some it's as simple as eating a piece of chocolate and drinking some water. Others like to rub salt or earth into their hands. Find something that works for you to really bring you back into your physical body and everyday awareness.

- Keep your home and work spaces energetically as clear as you can. There are incense and smudge mixes that are good for this, but if that is not possible, then certain sounds can help, such as a ritual bell or singing bowl. If you use a healing system such as Reiki, this can also be used to clear spaces. Salt also has protective qualities and is used to mark barriers.

- You can also use protective symbols and objects around the home to prevent unwanted energy entering.

It should be made clear that very little will protect you from faery energies if you do get on the wrong side of them. Iron is effective, but they will simply wait until you don't have it on you. The best protection against faeries is to remain on their good side and leave those that do not wish to be disturbed alone. They are unlikely to seek you out to cause trouble unless you have done something to disturb them first.

Cherry of Zennor (Cornwall)

Cherry of Zennor is an unusual tale as it is a female protagonist taken into Faery by a male initiating figure as opposed to the more common male protagonist led or taken into Faery by a faery woman. This story contains some key elements of Faery lore, including shapeshifting, apples as a fruit of otherworldly knowledge, and the crossroads as a meeting place between the worlds...

Cherry was a bright and energetic teenage girl who lived with her mother and father and numerous brothers and sisters in a small house with only two rooms in which they all lived together. While they were all healthy and had enough to eat, Cherry would see girls her own age from other families being given fancy dresses with bright ribbons by their sweethearts, and she wanted nice things for herself. She resolved to leave home and seek her fortune, packing up a small amount of belongings in a bundle and setting out in search of employment. She would buy her own dresses!

Though she promised her concerned relatives and friends that she would not travel too far afield, she wandered so far south that by the end of the day she found herself in altogether unfamiliar territory. She sat down at a crossroads and cried. After resting there awhile, she resolved in her tears to return and make the best of her life at home. However, she was surprised to find that when she looked up from her tears there was a handsome, well-dressed gentleman looking down and offering her a concerned hand. When she explained that she had left home looking for work, he declared it excellent fortune, as he had been looking for a young lady just like her to enter service at his home to look after a child (as he had recently been made a widower) and milk the cow. The gentleman appeared kind and charming and was obviously of no mean wealth, so she agreed to accompany him to his residence and enter his employment.

They walked for many hours, but Cherry found she quite lost track of time in his charming company. They walked down a lane lined with apple trees heavy with fruit and the scent of honeysuckle.

* * *

The path grew very thick with trees, so she could no longer see sunlight, and it became denser and darker the further they went on. When they came across a clear stream, the gentleman carried Cherry across it easily, and soon she found that they were in the most beautiful gardens she ever could have imagined, full of bright colours and delights that filled her senses. Before them was a gate and a lovely house, and the gentleman told Cherry that this was where he lived.

Out of the gate appeared a beautiful child with strangely piercing eyes that seemed wise beyond his years. After him came an old and haggard woman, who shot Cherry a dark look and took the child inside the house. This filled Cherry with some trepidation until the gentleman explained that this was his late wife's grandmother and that she would only stay on to teach Cherry what she needed to know and then would leave.

Cherry was well fed and went to rest, being instructed by the old woman, Prudence, not to open her eyes or poke about at night lest she see things that were not her business. The next day she received her instructions as to what her work would entail. She was to bathe the child in a spring in the garden and anoint his eyes with a special ointment that was kept in a crystal box, and she must be absolutely certain not to get even a tiny amount on her own eyes. Then she was to milk the cow, give the boy the milk for his breakfast, and not ask questions.

Of course, Cherry was full of lively curiosity, but whenever she started to question the child, he threatened to tell the old woman, and her fear of Prudence kept her silent for a while. She dutifully bathed the boy and anointed his eyes, then called the cow and milked her. The milk flowed readily, the boy was fed, and Cherry herself was given a delicious and filling breakfast.

After completing her work well for the first day and dutifully suppressing her curiosity, on the second day her master praised her work and gave her more tasks, such as picking fruit in the garden, and he would always give her a loving kiss to show how pleased he was with her. After a few days, Prudence led Cherry down a long, dark passage to areas of the house she had been forbidden to enter by her master. They came to a room that looked to be made of glass, full of what appeared to be small stone figures. Cherry had started to suspect she might be in fairyland and was now afraid she had come to the house of a dangerous conjurer where she too might be turned to stone. Prudence then ordered her to scrub at a coffin-like box until it shone, deriving some sadistic pleasure from Cherry's fear, until her master found them and admonished the old woman for taking Cherry into the forbidden places of the house. He took Cherry back to the kitchen and helped her back to her senses, always being kind and loving to her.

· · ·

The old woman had now gone and Cherry passed a year in the gentleman's service as though it was a day, but soon she could no longer fight her curiosity, convinced she could sometimes hear him talking to the stone people in the hidden room. That day, after anointing the child's eyes, she placed a small amount of the forbidden ointment on her own eye, which burned so painfully she went to wash it off in the spring—but when she looked into the spring, there she saw her master, shrunk to a tiny size and dancing with little people!

Cherry tried to carry on as usual all day, but when her master got back from hunting that evening, she heard beautiful music coming from his rooms and peeked through the keyhole. There she saw him kissing a beautiful lady in a green dress and was overcome with jealousy. When he went to kiss Cherry at the end of the day for her good work, she slapped him and told him to save his kisses for the lady in green. Now her master was filled with sadness as he knew she had gone against his wishes and used the ointment on herself. She would have to leave, but he might visit her again one day if she was good.

As the sun rose, Cherry found herself back at the crossroads, with no sign of the garden or the gentleman, and though she found her way home, she was never the same again, always longing after the beautiful land and love that she once knew.

Sometimes lying on the hillside with the eyes of the body shut as in sleep, I could see valleys and hills, lustrous as a jewel, where all was self-shining, the colours brighter and purer, yet making a softer harmony together than the colours of the world I know.

George William Russell,
The Candle of Vision

The Sacred Landscape

It is of utmost importance to keep your awareness of Faery grounded in the natural world around you as much as possible. Once you have performed the exercises from the book so far a number of times, you should have developed your sensitivity enough to start to sense the places in the landscape where our realm and the realm of Faery naturally overlap.

Faery Landmarks

Here are some suggestions of great starting points in nature to build awareness and connect with the Faery realm. If you have any of the following landmarks near you or are able to visit them, spend time there performing both the Faery Tree exercise and contemplations of the elements, and then sit with the expanded awareness and stillness and see what (or who) makes themselves known to you.

Trees

In our underworld journey, we have already touched on the idea that trees, especially those with obvious gateways such as hollows between roots, can offer a connection with and entrance to the Faery realm. In many ways, they are a bridge between ourselves and the Faery races, an in-between point. They resemble us in their physical structure (as we have explored in the Faery Tree exercise), and when we are sensitive to their energies, we often find trees with particular personalities. Other trees have more of a "hive mind" consciousness, connected by their roots. Spending time in the company of trees that we feel magnetically drawn to can open us up to contact with faery beings, especially nature spirits and the spirits that dwell in trees and are their guardians, such as dryads.

Trees that have strong associations with Faery are:

Alðer: A protective, warrior-like energy, strong willed.

Apple: *Avalon* means "Isle of Apples," and in ballads such as "Thomas the Rhymer," apples are seen to grow on trees in the Faery underworld. They are particularly associated with healing, wisdom, and feminine energy. Apple is connected with the energies of faery queens.

Ash: Ash has qualities of strength, resilience, and protection, and it is strongly connected to traditionally masculine energies such as the Horned God and faery kings.

Beech: Beech trees can act as powerful gateways to Faery and aid seekers of knowledge and wisdom. They have a strong serpent energy, connecting to the currents of the underworld.

Birch: A bright energy connected with new beginnings and rebirth, it can aid in traveling between worlds and also for protection.

Blackthorn: Connected with the darker side of Faery energy and often used for cursing and deep magic.

Elder: This tree is connected with powers of shapeshifting, and the spirits of this tree are often shapeshifters themselves.

Hawthorn: One of the most important trees in Faery lore, it is the brighter sister to blackthorn. When the flowers of the hawthorn blossom, they herald the festival of Beltane, one of the times of year when the world of Faery may be most powerfully perceived.

Hazel: When two hazel trees grow together, they form a powerful gateway to Faery. Hazel is also associated with eloquence and divination.

Holly: A strong, bright energy, this evergreen is linked to old magic and warrior spirits.

Oak: One of the most powerful and individual trees, oak is closely connected to the father god of the Sidhe, the Dagda, and to the Green Man. Large oaks in an area often will be home to the guardian spirit of that place.

Rowan: A powerful Faery tree with solar associations, rowan protects against negative energies and influences.

Willow: Very connected to lunar and watery energies, willow is connected to the deep emotional side of Faery. Willow can help with healing and opening up empathic communication with the Faery realm.

Yew: Associated with death due to its toxic properties, yew can be an overwhelmingly powerful tree for Faery work. However, this tree plugs deeply and directly into Faery, enabling you to hear the drumbeat of the earth if you can still yourself. Deep transformations come from working with the spirit of yew.

Ancient Woods and Forests

Places where ancient woodland remains undisturbed can be difficult to find, depending on where in the world you are, but if you are lucky enough to have access to such a primal location, to sit in silence and open awareness there may lead to special encounters. The more you build up a relationship with the spirits of place by proving yourself trustworthy, connecting through song and/or offerings (more on this in later chapters), the more you will build your connection, open your senses, and find yourself able to perceive and communicate with the power and beings within the land.

Hedgerows

The liminal nature of hedgerows as boundary keepers and the fact that they are a habitat for abundant and varied life makes them a natural crossover point for faery encounters. Indeed, folklore is full of tales of the kinds of prickly beings that are associated with these tangles of thorns and leaves. While this is a powerful place to connect, be ready to deal with some of the tricksier characters amongst our cousins, and practice answering riddles!

Hills

Hills are also a liminal location, where land and sky meet. Folklore, myth, and lived mystical experience teach us that the faery nobility live within the hollow hills, and even if we may not have a hill near us with specific folklore attached to it, their presence can be felt. Is there a hill that you feel inexplicably drawn to or that somehow pulls your attention towards it whenever you drive by? Just as some people have more natural charisma than others, so certain locations in the landscape have a natural magnetism, as though the inner earth sings out from that point. If you have a hill that you can visit, spend some time sitting in silent contemplation there or perhaps offer a song and see what comes to you.

Standing Stones

Built by our ancient ancestors to mark the seasons in places of power on the landscapes, standing stones and circles of stones are a potent point of connection between the realms. Most of us are not lucky enough to live in close proximity to such locations, but you may have the opportunity to visit. Stone circles will have guardian stones that act as a gateway, and it is also important to greet the spirits of place respectfully. If you are uncertain of which stones seem to be the entrance point, do a full clockwise circuit of the stones and, when you feel drawn to do so, enter in humility and gratitude. To sit quietly with your back against a standing stone, especially in the peace of a starlit night, is to feel true connection between above, below, and within.

Natural Gateways

Gateways that have naturally formed in nature are excellent locations to pass into otherworldly awareness. Look for powerful pairs of trees that grow together in the landscape and seem to offer a portal that you can pass through (all the more powerful if they are trees with a strong connection to Faery, such as oak, ash, or hawthorn). Other examples of natural gateways include locations where a hole has been naturally worn through rock, such as rock archways or caves. As natural underworld entrances, caves can be a particularly powerful place to make contact with the living inner world.

EXERCISE

Stepping Through the Gateway

Approach the gateway with reverence, greeting the spirits and guardians of place. If you do not feel able to vocalise this due to there being other people present, keep your focus on your intent and internalise it; your intent will be felt.

Stand at the entrance of the gateway and see if you can perceive any shift in the atmosphere; you may even perceive a slight distortion from one side of the gateway to the other. Extend your inner senses to connect with the energy of the gateway and ask for permission to pass through. If you feel it is granted, stand within the gateway with your arms extended, palms outward, sensing the shift between the worlds. Close your eyes and breathe. Allow your perception to expand and be open to experience whatever wishes to present itself.

Spend some time in contemplation after passing through, but do remember to mark returning to your own realm afterwards—we all need to function in the human world!

Burial Mounds

The realm of Faery and burial mounds are inextricably linked, not least through the common name of Sidhe in Irish and Scottish lore. The most significant structures of this kind that we are aware of, such as Newgrange in Ireland, were built to align with the cycles of the year and the position of the sun, moon, and stars. These are places built by the ancestors to ease the passing of souls into the otherworld and are therefore, by their very nature, perfect places to make contact with faery beings. It is a powerful place to practice journey work in particular. However, if you choose to do so, it is important to equally honour the spirits of those who rest there and always ask permission of the guardians of place.

Lakes and Pools

Bodies of still water are nature's magic mirrors, especially at full moons, when the surface of the water looks almost like quicksilver. Lakes and pools often have their own folklore attached to them, such as Dozmary Pool in Cornwall, which is one of the sites strongly associated with the Lady of the Lake and Excalibur. Many faery queens and kings have their realms in lake depths such as these. Try practicing the Nimue guided meditation whilst you sit on the shore of a lake and see how vivid it becomes!

Wells and Springs

Wells and springs are often associated with healing powers, and though wells in particular often may be adopted as holy by the church, their sacredness predates the arrival of the Christian religion and saints. The healing power of these primal locations comes from the waters that bubble up from the underworld. If you are lucky enough to have an ancient well or spring near you, not only will it be a powerful point of contact between the realms, but the water will be helpful for use in any magical work.

The guardian spirits of wells and springs usually take the form of a white lady. We will look at offerings in more depth in the next chapter, but be sure not to leave anything unnatural or polluting at such sites. All wells are spiritually connected in the underworld and connect to the primal Grail energy. With experience you can learn to spiritually link to wells in other locations through a well that you are connected to. This is helpful not only in increasing your awareness of the interconnection of all things but also if there is any work that needs doing in areas you are not geographically near to.

Greeting Guardians

All places of power within the landscape will have guardians, and you may find your own places of connection in locations that don't conform to the above list; Faery isn't really about conformity, after all! These guardians may or may not be corporeal, so it is a good idea to have done the work to increase your empathic awareness and energetic sensitivity in order to be able to sense them when they present themselves. If you intend to do any spiritual or magical work on the site, they should be sought out and greeted first, their permission requested.

The nature of a guardian will tend to reflect the nature of the site, but it is best to be open to all possibilities rather than approach with expectations. An open heart, pure intent, and the demonstration of goodwill is all that is required. With these qualities and a polite request, it is unlikely that you will be refused. However, if you do sense that now is not the time or place for whatever reason, to proceed will be detrimental, and it is best to give respectful thanks and leave. Offerings may be given in order to build a relationship with a site guardian, and we will look in the next chapter at what is appropriate (and what is not).

Guardians will sometimes take the form of animals or birds, and you will quickly notice if there is such an animal acting strangely. Perhaps your path is being blocked by a horse or a goose, or perhaps even a wren or other small bird seems particularly attentive. Honour them in the same way: show humility and honourable intent, ask for permission to enter, and see what happens. Sensitivity to the energies of the landscape around you and your own relationship with and connection to the land is of key importance when working with Faery, and these locations where our worlds most strongly overlap are not always obvious.

Since we all have a unique energy signature, as well as a tendency to connect strongly with one element over others, we each may find our own special places in the landscape, be it rural or urban, to "plug in." Many known sacred sites can be very busy with tourists, so for work that requires peace and privacy, here is an exercise to help you find your own personal place of power within the landscape.

Walking in Awareness

When first performing this exercise, as a starting point, choose a location in nature where you will be mostly undisturbed (this could be a park if you live in a city or town and are unable to travel to the countryside).

To begin, perform the Faery Tree exercise, drawing energy from above and below to meet in your heart centre and form a swirling ball of golden energy. Now, rather than releasing that energy back, breathe into it and allow the golden light to expand and surround you. Keeping your breathing steady, visualise golden tendrils of energy reaching out from your centre and into the landscape around you.

It may be wise, if you are a beginner, to just focus on this stage for your first few attempts and see how the tendrils allow you to connect with the spirit of plants, trees, and other living things around you, including rocks and the land itself. Can you feel a response from the life you reach with your golden tendrils of light? You may feel that experiencing this is enough for now (in which case, retract the tendrils and release energy back to above and below as in the Faery Tree exercise) or after some practice you may feel ready to start moving forward into the landscape. Remember, keep yourself safe. This is about expanding awareness, paying real attention to the world around you, not having your head in the clouds and tripping over roots or falling off anything!

Allow the tendrils to guide you as you explore the landscape, your energetic sensitivity heightened. Which direction do you feel drawn to move in? Do you perceive any shifts in energy around you? Is a feature in the landscape or a particular area calling to you? It may be that you do not have to move far, but if you do, try not to get too lost (though my best adventures have often involved getting just lost enough).

Allow all your senses to take in every bit of information: the buzzing of an insect, the rustling of leaves in the wind. Feel the bark of trees; allow scents on the breeze to move you. Savour the moment. It may be that you find a place that runs through you like electricity, or you may simply find peace and oneness in the moment. Your experience will be yours and no one else's.

You may set a slightly different intent for this exercise, such as making contact with a new ally or receiving an oracular message from nature. Once you feel your experience is concluded, return to your starting point and close down as in the Faery Tree exercise, releasing the energy back to above and below. Repeat in different locations and see what adventures and experiences present themselves.

Urban Awareness

When you're confident you can use this technique and not appear like a visitor from outer space walking down the street, it can be really rewarding to keep this level of awareness during a walk through a city. Secret gems of spaces can reveal themselves. Oracular messages appear in shop signs and snatches of overheard conversation. Only try this when you're sure you can tune in without stepping in front of a bus, though, please!

It can feel much more challenging to contact Faery whilst surrounded by the noise, bustle, and abundance of confusing energies in the city, but wherever there is life, there is Faery. These places were not always built up, and many may one day return again to their natural state. Faeries exist alongside us on a different resonance, and although some are very much rooted in place, there are ancestral faery beings that appear to travel with humans as they have colonised various areas of the world. These kinds of beings are quite at home in cities and may be frequently detected once you have learned to tune in to them. For example, the artist Brian Froud talks about having seen leprechauns frequently on the streets of locations in the States where there is a large population of people with Irish ancestry.

Equally, whilst some faery beings are very much rooted in particular places in the landscape, some may travel with you. Either way, if they are approached in honour and friendship and you prove that you are able to keep your side of any arrangement, strong connections can be formed with Faery wherever you are in the world.

The Roots Beneath
the City Visualisation

This simple visualisation is specifically for those who live in urban areas and feel that disconnection from nature is blocking them from connecting with Faery.

You can perform this visualisation at home. Find a time and place where you can sit comfortably and not be disturbed. Close your eyes and take three deep breaths in and out, releasing the cares and worries of the day with each exhale. Picture the room that you are sitting in now in as much detail as you can manage. Allow your awareness to sink into the floor beneath you and the walls around you. Know that the materials all around you consist of the four elements: earth, air, fire, and water. All is part of nature.

Let your awareness continue to journey through the walls and however many floors are beneath you until you reach the ground. Know that this foundation is strong and supports you, and also know that even a small weed has the power to push *through concrete. You notice one such weed: it has a bright white flower with seven petals and seems to glow. Allow your awareness to merge into the weed and then move downward through its roots into the earth. Now you are surrounded by a network of roots from plants and trees. There are even some creatures burrowing here. Everything is vibrant and pulsing with energy. You join the flow of this energy for a while and notice there are faery beings here with you too as part of the growth and vitality that exists within the whole world. You see one great root in front of you and follow it down into a green light that seems to grow in intensity as you approach, until your whole sight is filled with green.*

Your eyes adjust to the light and you find yourself within a beautiful landscape, the primal land of Faery. You are at peace here and feel an energy of renewal surge inside of you. You are aware of yourself as part of nature, and that as part of nature yourself, you carry this land inside of you, just as the land does. All the paths down the roots of the world lead to this same realm at the centre, no matter the landscape of the surface. When you feel ready, allow your awareness to rise back up through the roots, back up through the same weed pushing its way through the concrete, back through the floors and walls of your building, back to where you are seated.

Bring your awareness fully back into yourself: feel your fingers, your toes. Feel your breath. Feel the energy of Faery still in your centre. Take three deep breaths once more and open your eyes when you are ready. Eat and drink something to ground yourself back in your body.

Tam Lin (Scotland)

Tam Lin (much like Thomas the Rhymer, which comes from roughly the same geographical area, the Scottish borders) is an extremely important traditional initiatory ballad, all the more so for showing a young girl in a heroic role. The rose is a key symbol within Faery initiatory paths, and its presence here as a trigger for Tam Lin's appearance is very significant. The theme of shapeshifting is central once again, and there is much symbolism (including the replacement of body parts), which may be encountered in shamanic-style journey work. It is also important to note that Janet is aware of the tales behind the warnings and chooses the action that will lead to her entry into the Faery mysteries…

．．．

A long time ago, in the borderlands of Scotland, a king forbade all maidens of the land to visit the forest of Carterhaugh, for there dwelled a mysterious being known as Tam Lin, who might steal the ring that ties back their hair, their dresses, or their maidenhood!

This warning didn't quite have the effect that the king intended, for a young woman called Janet ran to Carterhaugh with her green skirt tucked up so she could run all the faster (green is the colour of the fairies, so she knows what she's doing) and, quite willing to part from her maidenhood, plucked the forbidden rose that was said to summon Tam Lin. Tam Lin did indeed appear, and very handsome he was too! He scolded Janet for pulling the forbidden rose, and she willingly gave up her maidenhead to him in return.

Some months passed, and it became clear that Janet was pregnant and that Tam Lin was the father, so she returned again to Carterhaugh and gathered herbs that would make her lose the baby. Tam Lin appeared again and asked her not to harm the child. She took this opportunity to ask him who he was and where he came from, to which he replied that he was a human knight that had been kidnapped by the queen of Faery when he fell off his horse whilst hunting. He went on to say that although Faeryland was a beautiful place, they had a custom of making sacrifices to hell every seven years, and he feared that this time he would be the one sacrificed.

Tam Lin told Janet that if she wished to rescue him, so that her child may have a father, the following night, Halloween, was when the sacrifice was planned. She must let pass a brown horse and a black horse, but he would be on a white horse, and she must pull him from the horse and hold onto him no matter what.

The night came and she bravely did as he had asked, holding onto him even though the faeries changed his shape—from a lion to red-hot metals—until he was restored to his true form and she had to cover him in her mantle.

Through her strength and bravery, Janet is victorious, winning him back from the Faery queen, who admired her courage but said that if she had known what was going to happen, she would have turned his heart to stone and replaced his eyes with wood.

The nature of those spirits, or Elves, is they are affected with and Love all those that Love them, & hate all those that hate them; yea they Know both our mind & thoughts in a great measure, whereby it comes to pass, that we may Easily Move them to come to us, if we rightly understand the rules thereof…

Sloane MS 3825 (a seventeenth-century grimoire)

CHAPTER

5

Honouring the Heart of Faery

Honour is a quality that is rarely spoken of these days, and yet it is something we could all do with prioritising in our dealings with the world, with each other, and with spiritual beings such as faeries. First, let us shed any thoughts of honour being confused with glory, as it tends to be, along with associations with victory in battle and various other scenarios that come down to obeying orders and risking your life for a supposed great cause. When we talk about honour

in a spiritual and magical context, we mean establishing a strong code of ethics and sticking to it, even when (especially when) that is difficult. To live in an honourable way is to walk in our own truth, and this is something that faery beings can sense and will respect. The double meaning of honour relates to how we honour our faery allies and other beings that we meet, and throughout this chapter we will look at various ways we can live in an honourable relationship with Faery, as well as ways to deepen our connection.

Walking in Honour

No one can dictate to you what your personal code of honour should be; that is for you to find and decide for yourself. Spend some time in contemplation of how you wish to move through the world. Write down your principles and vow to abide by them. If you apply a certain code to one part of your life, have you also applied it to the rest? There are certain qualities, which we have already discussed, that will be required of you in order to build a relationship with Faery, and it is important to keep them both in your spiritual work and your everyday dealings. The path of Faery is not confined to whatever time you set aside for it; it will permeate all aspects! However chaotic that may seem at times, if you work harmoniously and honourably with them, your life will be transformed for the better.

Faery Etiquette

The following points are a mixture of wisdom gained from folklore, experience, and common (or perhaps uncommon) sense. They will help as a starting point for you to build your own code of ethics and should help form healthy connections with the Faery realm.

Speak the Truth

Lying is a big no-no when dealing with faeries. If you carry any deception in your heart, even if it is in dealings with others and not with them, they will detect it and instantly distrust you. This may seem surprising when we consider the tricksy nature of many faeries in old tales (and indeed in experience), but that behaviour in itself is more complex than it appears on the surface. Mischievous and sometimes malicious actions can usually be attributed to the "solitary" type of faery being, such as pixies, goblins, etc., usually as either a conscious initiatory challenge to test our worthiness or as a kind of wake-up call to our own behaviours.

Sometimes things may go missing and reappear in odd places—they may be trying to get your attention or testing you to see if you have a sense of humour! However, they will not deceive you when you enter into a trusting and collaborative relationship with them; there will be some lesson behind it if something like this occurs. Darker behaviours such as those exhibited by unseelie beings should be taken as a warning. These beings do not desire to work with us as they have seen too much of the deception, destruction, and cruelty that humanity is capable of, and they should be avoided.

Iron

For hundreds of years people have been placing horseshoes above their doorways for luck, but originally this was to protect against devils, witches, and faeries, as it was a source of iron that people would easily have had access to. It is common folklore that faeries cannot abide iron, and in fact it is effective against other spiritual entities too, hence the tales in folklore of the devil being driven away by a horseshoe and why magical tools used in ceremonial magic for the command of spirits (rather than cooperation with) will usually contain iron. Iron and any metal that contains iron can cause harm to faery beings, and they will react poorly to you carrying it when seeking connection with them. However, it is worth remembering this if you ever find yourself in the unfortunate position of getting on the wrong side of any faery being or needing to protect yourself. Most people on magical paths who work with faery substitute wood or bronze tools for their magical work.

Faery Food

One of the best-known pieces of faery lore is that you should not eat any faery food, for if you do, various very unpleasant things will occur. In Christina Rossetti's 1862 poem "Goblin Market," two sisters are tempted by jewel-like fruit, and when one succumbs, she starts to waste away. She can no longer be sustained by human food and can no longer hear or see the goblins. Through the heroic aid of her sister, she is finally cured before she wastes away.

> *We must not look at goblin men,*
> *We must not buy their fruits:*
> *Who knows upon what soil they fed*
> *Their hungry thirsty roots?*
>
> Christina Rossetti, "Goblin Market"

Other tales tell of being trapped in Faery forever as a slave if you partake of the food. Certainly it is good to be wary! This should be maintained as a rule until such a time when you have reached a level of experience, trust with your allies, and wisdom that you see the point at which the rule can be broken.

Taking from Faery Sites

One of the many reasons for building a good empathic and intuitive connection with the landscape as a first step in Faery work is in order to avoid unintentional blunders such as accidentally taking something from a site sacred to Faery without permission. These sites are often unmarked in any way by humans; it is more likely that you will sense a shift in the atmosphere than any sign or guidebook will tell you of their location. Some examples are remembered in folklore, such as it being bad luck to bring a branch of hawthorn into the home, a tree sacred to Faery. One of the reasons they find it difficult to trust us is that humanity has a long track record of taking without permission or giving something of equal value in exchange.

In countries such as Ireland and Iceland, there is still so much of a living tradition connected to Faery (*Huldufólk,* or "hidden people," in Icelandic) that road planning will still take into account the places that belong to them and must not be disturbed, including moving stones from their land. You will still see the occasional headline in newspapers today about people who have met with ill fortune that is 100 percent put down to crossing the faeries! Once you have expanded and deepened your connection with your allies and the inner landscape, you will be able to sense if you are allowed over boundaries to take stones or branches and what might be an acceptable exchange.

Giving Thanks

There is a theme that runs through a number of faery and folk tales that you should never thank faeries for work or favours they do for you, for if you do so, they will vanish and you will not see them again. My own theory is that this is due to a misinterpretation on both sides. To simply thank them for something they have done may be considered dismissive and final. We should always be grateful, but it is more in the spirit of a reciprocal relationship and continued collaboration to ask what we can do in return. We should certainly never take them for granted or consider them in any way "our little helpers."

Offerings

We've touched on this subject a few times already, so let's now look at offerings in more depth. Offerings are a great way of building a relationship with any spiritual entity, including faeries and spirits of place. But why? A good offering, when it is accepted, is a direct exchange of energy between yourself and the otherworldly being in question. It may also seal a promise or be a concrete representation of an intent. If you bear this in mind, then it is easy to work out what makes a good or bad offering, knowing that the more it is energetically unique or meaningful to you, the better the intent behind it and the more effective it will be in building your connection with the Faery realm. It goes without saying that offerings should not have any negative environmental impact, nor should they interfere with the energy of the place where they are being offered. Here are some simple examples of good ways to make offerings:

Song

Using your voice is the most direct way of offering and connecting your energy to Faery, and it has the added bonus of not leaving any waste material behind! Your voice is an expression of your soul's unique energy signature, and no skill is required in offering a song, be it learned or improvised in the moment. Your voice will carry the energy of your intent, and as long as your intent is pure, that is what counts. However, you will find (as with any skill) that the more you practice and can lose any inhibitions, the more your voice will reflect your inner self. There is an exercise in the next chapter to help you with this. With experience you may find, as I have, that certain melodies will come to you in channeling, meditation, or journey work that can act specifically as bridges or invocations to faery beings and their realm.

Music

For those who have the skill or are willing to take the time to learn it, a small portable instrument is a wonderful thing to take out into nature. Faeries love all creativity, so this is another great way to show your love and respect for them. If you have any skill in composition, this would be especially appreciated, and you may find faery allies joining you to inspire more musical creations.

Dance

If you cannot create your own music, try tuning into their music, to the frequencies of the inner landscape, and see if it moves you to dance. Bringing those sensations into expression through the body, no matter your physical limitations, will help make your connection stronger and more grounded. Again, it is not skill but the open heart and intent that count—to dance without fear, to move with the love of nature and our faery cousins.

Cream or Milk

A bowl of cream or full cream milk is a traditional offering to the faery folk, especially domestic sprites such as brownies, and they must always be given the top of the milk, the creamiest portion. This is often done at a full moon, as the round bowl of milk reflects the image of the moon. This is perhaps not one for the vegans amongst us, and considering the current state of the dairy industry, you may want to think about the welfare of any animals involved before you use it as an offering. The tradition of offering milk dates from a time when people lived and farmed in more harmonious relationship with nature and gave a portion of their produce to keep their faery allies on their side. If you happen to know (or even be) an organic dairy farmer and milk is part of your life, and you treat the animals responsibly, then this might still be a good way to go. On the other hand, I don't recommend using store-bought soya or almond alternatives. Consider the many other options from this chapter as offerings instead.

Alcohol

Alcohol is a universally popular offering and is especially appropriate for Faery work as it is the result of a collaboration between nature and humanity, with nature producing the fruit or grain and then our human process of fermenting to create the alcohol. Red wine is a powerful choice, as this connects to the rivers of blood that Thomas the Rhymer must wade through to access Faery and is the drink that is offered to him by the faery queen. Cider is also sacred to Faery, as apples grow on the Isle of Avalon and again are an important part of Faery wisdom. If you share a drink with the faeries, be sure to offer them the first portion and not just what you have left over!

Baked Goods

Again, baking is a product of nature plus our processes, and the inherent energy of bread or cakes can be used by Faery or consumed by them in animal form. If you love to bake, this is a wonderful way to make offerings, as the energy you put into creating it makes it all the more acceptable. Be mindful not to include ingredients like chocolate or anything artificial that might be harmful to animals, and always clear away any remnants the next day. If you're not one of life's bakers (I'm not!), then consider what your own strengths are and what might be more appropriate. Something that comes from you personally will be better than anything you just buy in a shop.

Incense

Carefully selected resins or herbs burnt on a charcoal disc in a safe container make an excellent offering. Be sure to never leave it burning unsupervised, however! If you are lucky enough to have a garden, you may wish to grow your own herbs specifically for this purpose, which you can then dry and blend yourself with magical intent. There are also companies that sell hand-blended magical incenses, so do a bit of research and see if you can find an ethical company that is convenient for you. Of course it is also okay to use stick incense, but try to be aware of the quality of ingredients. Again, always be sure to clear away any remnants.

Flowers

Though flowers are often used on shrines or as offerings, consider deeply their source and appropriateness. Does picking wildflowers and essentially killing them make a worthy gift? Consider planting wildflower seeds instead. Fragrant herbs grown in your own garden that you can harvest without harming are an excellent alternative.

Acts of Devotion

It is a good idea to prove that you are willing to walk the talk by performing dedicated acts such as clearing litter from a local park, planting trees, or planting wildflower seeds—anything that benefits your local environment. Sometimes your faery allies will request such acts from you in exchange for their assistance and guidance. It is a really good way to show that your intents are selfless and that you can follow through on promises.

Creative Acts

It is a natural impulse of a liberated human soul to create, whether that be through writing, drawing, painting, dance, drama, sculpture, or photography. Whatever your outlet is, that means you can produce something unique to you to give as an offering, something that thought and heart have gone into. Whether it be ephemeral and gone in a moment or something that lasts and continues to act as a bridge between worlds, any offering that could only come from you is the best kind.

Avoid…

Here are some big no-nos:

- Chocolate is toxic and even deadly to many animals and must under no circumstances be left outdoors in nature.

- Glitter is tiny bits of plastic. It looks pretty but is actually really bad for the environment. Edible and hence biodegradable alternatives are now available if you really need the effect!

- Leftovers. Always give the first and best portion; anything else is offensive.

- Ethically sourced crystals may be used in your own home and in your spiritual practice, but leaving them at sacred sites, no matter how well meaning, is actually polluting the natural energy of the place and muddies the natural flow.

- Plastic clooties. A clootie is a strip of cloth tied onto a branch at a sacred site, usually a well, to pray for healing. The meaning seems to have been lost to quite a few people, who have taken to tying all sorts of nonsense onto branches, including strips of artificial cloth and plastic. If you come across these anywhere, please clear them. While the intent may be good, the thought is sadly lacking, and the effect is contrary to what may be desired.

EXERCISE

Making an Offering

For those who are just starting out on the Faery path and would
like some guidance on how to make offerings, here are some clear
steps to follow...

Choosing/Creating the Offering

The previous list should give you plenty of ideas, and any of these
suggestions would work well as offerings, but to make it extra
effective in building your personal connection with Faery, consider what you could offer that is uniquely you. If there is any
process of effort and creation that goes into it, that will contain
your energy signature and serve not only as a gift that shows
your good intent but also as a bridge that helps to align your
energy with the frequency of the faery beings you wish to work
with. There is more guidance to help you unlock your gifts and
create offerings from your soul later in this book.

Timing

To build a strong relationship with Faery, it is best to leave regular offerings. As with most Faery work, so long as principles are adhered to, there is no set structure, but once a month is good practice, particularly at a full moon. There are times of the year that are particularly associated with Faery, such as Beltane/Mayday, Midsummer, and Samhain/Halloween. More suggestions of how to celebrate these festivals are included later in the book.

Place

If you're lucky enough to have a garden, set aside a small area or shrine within it where you can leave your offerings. Even if you have a garden, there may be a different green space where you feel the energies are strong and resonate with you. Just be sure to leave it as you would wish to find it and treat it with respect, always clearing away any remains the next day.

Make Your Offering

While pomp and ceremony is not required, neither is it most effective to nip out to the garden and simply slosh a bottle of wine over your lawn! With all of the above stages taken into consideration, draw up a plan of what, when, and where you wish to make your offering.

When you arrive at the place you have chosen (even if it's just your backyard), take time to tune into the energy of place and allow your senses to take in everything around you. Now expand that awareness to include the inner landscape. I would advise performing the Faery Tree exercise to do this.

Once you are connected, reach out with your awareness and vocalise your intent. This helps focus your energy and also acts as an invocation to call on the energies and beings you wish to make your offering to so that they are aware of you and present. With experience and confidence, you will be able to write your own declaration or simply come up with something in the moment. (Some offerings, such as a song, may not require it.) Here is a version for those who would like a starting point:

Spirits of this place,
dwellers in the hollow hills,
shining guardians of the inner realm,
I greet you with an open
heart and pure intent,
Accept this, my offering, in
love and friendship
that we may walk the path together,
by the stars above and below,
in truth, in honour, and in love.

If your offering is a physical object of some sort, hold it up to the sky and then present it to the ground. Take as much time as you wish to be in the energy of the moment before grounding and returning to your daily life or moving on to any other work you wish to do afterwards.

Your Faery Shrine

The concept of a shrine might have connotations of worship or religion, but when working with Faery it is much more about having a focal point for your energetic connection. Be aware that this goes both ways, so if possible make your main shrine outdoors; if it must be inside, keep it away from any electrical equipment! Faery activity can cause chaos with technology, but technology also can interfere with the energy as well as the kind of natural connection and calm you need for Faery work.

Much like offerings, beyond following the basic principles of avoiding polluting or unnatural materials, etc., there are no particular rules for how your shrine should look. It should be a unique expression of your connection to Faery and will of course be subject to your life circumstances. Some of you will perhaps share a living space with someone who does not share your beliefs, others may have limited space but understanding people around them, and others may find themselves with both ample space and freedom of expression.

Building Your Shrine

Your shrine can be as small or as large as suits your circumstances, and it will build up over time as you add objects from nature or decorations to it. You should choose one central object to act as your main focus, usually an image, symbol, symbolic object, or statue. Many people choose to have representations of the four elements and/or hallows on their shrines, and if you start to use any tools in your work, these can also live here. This is a good argument for maintaining both an indoor and outdoor shrine if you can manage it, since certain objects will obviously perish outdoors and you may wish to have sacred space set aside indoors for those. Somewhere you can safely burn candles and incense is also usual.

Blessing Your Shrine

From the journey work earlier in this book, you should have connected with and started to form a bond with a faery ally. Call upon them to help you bless your shrine so it can act as a focus for your mutual collaboration, and ask what objects they would like to have included. If your shrine is outdoors, you can share some wine or mead with your faery ally, pouring some onto the ground as a libation offering. If you are able to include representations of the four elements, you can use each in turn to bless your shrine: incense for air, a candle for fire, any stone or literally earth for earth, and a chalice or bowl of water, which you can sprinkle on the shrine in blessing. See if your ally can help you find wording for your blessing; otherwise, something as simple as the following will work:

> **I call upon my faery ally, the spirits of
> this place, and on the elements of earth,
> fire, air, and water to bless this shrine and
> our future work so that we may walk the
> path together in truth, honour, and love.**

Melusine (France)

Melusine is one of the most iconic examples of the faery bride who brings happiness but with a condition that must be kept secret. Of course the promise in these tales is always broken, with much sadness and loss ensuing. There is an important lesson in these tales about keeping promises and remaining honourable in all dealings with our faery allies. We must be trustworthy and also, crucially, trust them...

Melusine was one of triplets born to the faery woman Pressyne and the Scottish king Elynas. The three daughters grew up on the hidden Isle of Avalon with their mother, for when they were born, the king had accidentally broken a promise never to look in

● ● ●

on his wife in her chamber when she was sleeping in late, as he was so excited to see his children born. When the three sisters turned fifteen, their mother told the story of their father's broken promise, and Melusine decided to punish him. Along with her sisters, Melusine used their combined magic to imprison her father and his riches in a mountain. This angered their mother, for though she had been forced to leave him forever due to the broken promise, she still loved him. Pressyne placed a curse on Melusine that every Saturday she would become a serpent from the waist down, and the only way to break the curse would be to find a husband who would be able to keep a promise never to see her on a Saturday.

Melusine found her husband one day as she danced by the Fountain of Thirst in the forest. Raymondin had accidentally killed his uncle, the Count Aimery, whilst hunting boar in the forest, and Melusine helped him conceal his guilt and agreed to marry him. Her faery magic and wealth built a magnificent kingdom, which they ruled together.

Every Saturday she would keep to herself and take on her serpent form in secret. Even when their children were born with strange features, all was well between them until a relative of Raymondin planted a seed of jealousy in his mind, suggesting that the reason

• • •

she asked for privacy on a Saturday was that she was having an affair. He could not help himself and had to peek through the keyhole, where he saw her in her cursed form. He kept this to himself, as still he loved her and did not wish to lose her (or her wealth), until one day he was enraged at the destructive actions of one of their sons and called her a serpent in front of the whole court. With great sadness, she declared that she must now leave, and they were both condemned to walk in grief for the rest of their lives.

Syne they came on to a garden green,
And she pu'd an apple frae a tree—
"Take this for thy wages, true Thomas,
It will give the tongue that can never lie."

. . . .

Sir Walter Scott, "Thomas the Rhymer"

Unlocking
Your Gifts

It should be becoming clear by now that connecting to and working with Faery is at least as much about self-knowledge and your own inner journey as it is about anything exterior. After all, the better we know ourselves and the more work we do in identifying and working on our strengths and weaknesses, the better we will be able to keep grounded and sane as we venture into deeper and transformative connections with the beings of the inner world. In this chapter we will work on finding where our gifts lie and unlocking them so we can be free in our expression and open in our hearts in a way that encourages and strengthens Faery contact.

You Are Unique

The particular combination of genetics, brain chemistry, and life experience that make up "you" is an entirely unique phenomenon in space and time. There has only ever been, and will only ever be, one "you." Add to this the most important aspect, your spirit, and just think how potent that is!

All of us have been through experiences that have given us knocks and sometimes made us feel as though we may not have

much to offer, and this can cause blocks to our creativity and expression. As spiritual beings living a physical life, we are here to experience and create. Creation and imagination are not only essential to our spiritual health, they are the soul's language, and no two individuals are the same! It is a waste of energy (and also very blocking) to compare ourselves to others in this way. We move through the world in our own way, at our own speed and frequency, and just because your soul's expression may not fit some expectations does not make it less valid than another's. The following exercises are designed to help you develop modes of expression that will strengthen not only your ability to connect with Faery, but also to free your true self. These two things go hand in hand!

The Voice

Using your voice is one of the most direct ways to make energetic contact with the otherworld. Not only that, but with practice and the help of your allies, you can learn to use it as a tool for invocation (calling on spirits), healing, manifestation, or any other number of intents. In the last chapter we noted what an ideal offering a song from the soul can be. Your voice carries your unique energy signature into the world; paired with focused intent, it can be powerful indeed, opening gateways into Faery and aiding in communication with beings beyond words, directly connecting you heart to heart.

Freeing the Voice

The following exercises will help you gain awareness and control over your voice or, if you are already well versed in its use, help maintain your voice.

Finding the Diaphragm

Lie on your back with your knees raised and your feet flat on the floor (or the closest to this you can manage that is comfortable and practical). Rest your hands on your centre, just below your ribcage. Breathe deeply, right down into the bottom of your lungs, so it feels like you're breathing into your stomach and your back. Feel your hands raise and lower as you breathe in and out. Allow all tensions to melt away into the floor. As you continue to breathe deeply, work your way through every muscle, from the toes up, tensing it and then releasing it until you are completely relaxed. See how much you can expand your ribcage on each breath in and keep it expanded for as long as possible when breathing out, letting air leave the bottom of the lungs first.

Where your hands are resting, just below your ribcage, is a sheet of muscle called the diaphragm. Here is where all the support for the projection of your voice is really coming from, and rather than focusing on the throat, which can cause tensions and a lack of freedom, this is where your focus should be, as it also aligns with the energy centre of your solar plexus. (A really useful tip for opening your throat is to imagine you are yawning. Try yawning a few times before any vocal exercise.) On your next breath out, try a gentle pant and allow a "ha" sound to escape as you feel the diaphragm bounce. Increase to two on the next breath out—"ha ha"—and then three: "ha ha ha." Practice this until you can confidently feel the muscle working.

Resonating the Centre

Return once more to long, deep breaths, hand still on your centre. On your next breath out, allow sound to escape in a sustained hissing sound: "sssssss." Practice this and, without straining, see if you can extend the length of time you can sustain this sound.

Next, try an extended "fffffffff" and then "zzzzzzzz." With the "zzz" sound you can choose any note to sound, and you should start to feel it resonate around your face and perhaps in other parts of your head and body. Remember to try and keep the rib-cage expanded as long as possible for maximum resonance.

Once you have practiced this for a while, choose a note that feels comfortable and project it out towards the ceiling with a humming sound: "hmmmmm." Try different notes and pitches, exploring your full range. Where does it feel comfortable? Can you feel the note resonate through your body? In your centre? In your back? Where in your voice does it resonate most strongly and comfortably?

Experiment with humming up and down the scale to find where your voice naturally sits and vibrates.

Your True Note

There is no need to rush yourself. Practice the above exercises until you feel you have progressed to the point where you can feel your voice resonating, drawing from your centre, and you can hold a hummed note for a reasonable period of time.

Once more, lying on the floor with your knees raised, repeat all the above stages and come to a point where you have found a note that sits comfortably in your voice and that you can feel resonating in your centre. For two breaths, resonate this note on a hum. On the third, start with a hum, and once you feel the note vibrating in your centre, release it with an "ahhh" sound, opening your mouth and projecting the note upwards beyond the ceiling to the sky, allowing the sound to fill the room. Repeat three times.

Now slowly rise to a standing position (rolling onto your side and slowly curling upwards is advised). Stand with your feet directly below your hips, weight balanced evenly between them, back straight. Imagine your head suspended by a silver thread

from the heavens. If standing is not an option, then sit with your spine as straight as you can imagine, the energy flow from crown to root kept as clear as possible, a silver thread from the heavens suspending your head. Facing a wall, imagine a far horizon and a green landscape extending out in front of you. Repeat the exercise as before, remember to keep your ribcage expanded as much as possible, support your voice from your centre, and feel the note rise up from the floor, through your feet, up to your centre, and then out as any vowel sound through your throat and mouth, projecting it towards the horizon. Try not to let any tension sneak back in, especially into your throat—just let the note rise up and out, resonating in your body as it does so.

Everything in the universe has a resonant energy signature. Using your voice in this way directly connects your energy to the world around you and makes contact with faery beings, who will experience the intent sent with any note you resonate directly.

Using Your Voice in the World

Experiment with different vowel sounds. Are there sounds that make you think of a particular sort of landscape or element? If you are able to find outdoor locations where you will not feel too self-conscious, try tuning into your environment and allowing your voice to express instinctively the sensations and empathic impressions you are receiving. Now try combining this with the Faery Tree exercise. When the energy meets and becomes golden in your centre, allow that sensation to emerge in song, your voice and energy reaching out into the landscape. Let this sensation move your voice into a melody. Try not to be self-conscious about how it sounds; remember: it's more about the voice as vehicle for energy. However, the more you practice this, the more powerful, expressive, and confident your use of voice will become.

EXERCISE

Meeting the Piper
Guided Visualisation

Before starting this visualisation, make sure you have some method of recording your voice nearby (most smartphones will have a voice recorder app already installed) and, as usual, have a notebook and pen ready. Make sure you are sitting comfortably and upright, with your legs uncrossed and feet flat on the floor.

Close your eyes and take three deep breaths, releasing all the day's worries and tension on the out-breath. Visualise yourself in the room you are in now. As you keep your breathing steady, the room starts to fill with a white mist until all you see is white. With your next three breaths, the white mist clears and you find yourself at a crossroads in a green and wild place. To your left, which is the west, you see the path descend a hill down to the sea. To your right, the east, the path ascends into high mountains until it vanishes into clouds. Behind you, to the south, the green turns into sand, and a desert landscape stretches out into the distance. Before you the path winds into an ancient forest, the entrance marked with two moss-covered standing stones as a gateway. You hear music coming from the forest that seems to call you forward, so you follow the path into the forest, greeting the stones respectfully as you pass through them.

The forest feels welcoming and alive as you move deeper into it, always keeping to the path, and though you feel curious eyes and attention upon you, you feel quite safe as you follow the sound of the music, which seems to be being played on a pipe. You realise the forest seems to be lit with its own green light, and the sky above, which you can glimpse through the trees, is a luminous shade of purple.

After some time of following the music, you notice the path is widening. You step forward into a large clearing where all kinds of creatures are gathered around a large tree, whose trunk is wider than any you've seen in the forest thus far. Some are animals that you recognise; others are otherworldly, yet they all belong here. Faery beings of all kinds are gathered here to listen to the music. They welcome you as you step forward and see where the music is coming from.

A faun is sitting in the roots of the great tree, playing upon a pipe. As he notices you, he starts to play a short sequence of notes forming a melody that sounds as though it is meant specially for you. When he has played it through three times, you feel the urge to sing it back to him. As you do, you feel a surge of energy—light emanates from your centre, your heart, and your forehead. The sound and act of singing is attuning you to the frequency of Faery.

The piper is silent for a moment as you now sing the tune for the assembled crowd of faery beings, and they all sing with you. You realise you have an object in your right hand that represents your unique gift to the world. You step forward and present it to the piper as thanks for the song of connection and empowerment he has bestowed upon you.

When you are ready, you may bid farewell to the piper and the assembled beings and make your way back down the path through the forest to the crossroads. Do your best to hold onto the melody as the white mist appears. When the white mist clears, you are back in the room, and you may open your eyes, record your melody, and make any notes you wish. Be sure to have a drink of water and a bite to eat to ground yourself.

Words, Words, Words…

From Shakespeare and Spenser to Yeats and Tolkien, from the ancient ballads, myths, and folklore to today's fantasy films and TV shows, people have used words to express their devotion to the Faery realm and help others connect to a vision of the otherworld, just as I am doing now with this book!

Whether they believed in the truth of their vision, as visionary poets like Æ and Yeats did, or if they were creating a fantasy realm of escapism, words have always had the power to transport us. Poetry, song lyrics, stories, plays, educational resources…all can be acts of devotion and connection, and all can be inspired by Faery and inspire others to seek out that connection for themselves. You may or may not feel that you have a gift with words, but it is folkloric tradition that contact with the Faery realm can bring out this gift. Just as with the use of voice, your creativity with words doesn't necessarily have to be shared beyond yourself and your Faery contacts.

Seek Inspiration

Take some time to research poets and authors who have painted pictures of Faery with their words, and choose one who most inspires you. What is it about the way they use words that resonates with you? What is the rhythm of their writing? Try reading it aloud. How does it feel in the body? Combine with some of the vocal exercises in the previous section, choosing a line of text to resonate in the body. If you are able to do so, go out into nature and speak your chosen text to the trees, to the earth, to the sky, to the water. Listen with all your senses to see if there is any energetic response. Feel within yourself to see what the response is in your own physical, spiritual, and emotional body.

Carry a notebook with you. Do you feel moved to write your own words in response? Remember, no one is judging you. Try this with a few different writers' work and see how the response differs. How would you describe that in words? If you wished to create that response in others, how might you do that? Start with one word at a time and see what emerges. It might be one word, a line, a poem… let it build in its own time and take its form as it will. Allow words to flow through you without feeling the pressure to form them.

Clearing the Channel

Here are some quick and easy ideas for helping to unlock your inner wordsmith:

Print or write out a known poem, speech, or section of a book about Faery, and cut it into individual words and short phrases. Now rearrange at will and see what you can come up with. Try mixing them all in a bowl and picking at random. Do you get any meaning or message from them? How can you change or improve what you have? Use this as a starting point for inspiration and more creativity.

Find a peaceful spot to sit out in nature (a local park will do nicely) with your notebook or voice recorder. Relax and centre yourself. Let your senses settle on one detail that you notice: a tree, a flower, the sound of the wind, the heat of the sun. List some words that describe the sensations you feel when contemplating this detail. What words describe it physically?

Now, how does it behave? List words that describe its actions. Is it still or does it move? Consider all the senses and describe its effect on them. Does it move your spirit in any way? What is the personality or inner life of the detail you're describing? If it was a being, what kind of personality would it have? Where might it have been? Where might it be going next?

Now connect some of these words together and see what starts to form. A poem? A character? A story? Combined with exercises from the previous section, might you even have the makings of a song? Repeat as often as you like for other wonders of nature around you!

In the comfort of your home, cast your mind back to your experiences of the guided visualisations and journeys so far. Choose one to write up as a poem or story, describing it in as much detail as possible, as if it were to an artist so they could paint it for you.

The Mountain Sage
Guided Visualisation

Make sure you have a notebook or recording device ready for any notes you will need to make afterwards. Sitting comfortably in a place you will not be disturbed, legs uncrossed, close your eyes and take three deep breaths. Visualise yourself in the room, just as you are. With each breath out, release any concerns of the day. With each breath in, a white mist starts to fill your vision until it is completely white. Keeping your breathing steady, the white mist starts to clear, and you find yourself once more at the cross-roads, with the forest path ahead of you, the ocean path to the west, the desert path to the south, and the mountain path to the east. A cool and gentle breeze comes from the eastern path, and you turn to your right to face the mountain path.

Before you the path leads you towards a green mountain, winding up its great height until it seems to vanish into golden clouds. You cannot make out its peak. The air from that direction seems to whisper words to you in a language that your heart recognises, and you feel drawn to follow the path in that direction.

Though from the ground it appeared a great distance to the mountain, you find yourself winding up its slope much swifter than you might have imagined. The views of the sea, forest, and desert from your high vantage point make you feel inspired, and the whispered words on the breeze seem to grow in clarity as you keep moving higher up the path. As you continue upwards, you notice that the path is lined with rocks that seem to glisten and glitter in the golden light and bright yellow flowers amongst the long emerald grass, which delight your senses.

At what appears to be a halfway point, there is a tree with silver bark and a seat beneath, and you stop there for a brief rest. The breeze through the leaves of the tree sounds like gentle bells, and as you sit, three leaves fall into your lap. When you look closely at the leaves, you notice there are words written on them. You keep hold of these leaves, thanking the tree; when you are ready, continue on your journey.

You can now see the top of the mountain, and though you do not recall moving through mist, you are now looking down upon clouds. The path ahead climbs to a throne with a faery being sitting upon it. Upon closer inspection, you realise that the throne is made of books, and the faery being appears to be part owl. They peer at you intensely but not unwelcomingly. They speak: "Tell me, friend: What can you keep after you have given it to someone?"

You answer: "My word."

This appears to please the faery being, and they hold out a hand for you to place your leaves into. Try to remember the words that were written on them if you can. They look at the words on the leaves and speak them back to you. You feel a door within your mind open and know that when you return home, you will be able to write something that relates to these words. In return for your good answer and your gift of the leaves, they take a book from their throne and offer it to you. If you choose to accept the book, the being then says,

"Write the future you wish to see, create the person you wish to be, fill this book, and return to me..."

You open the book and see that it is empty but know you will be able to fill it with your own words. You may stay and talk further with the being if you wish.

When you are ready, you bid farewell to the sage and descend the path. If you wish to stop under the tree again, you may find more leaves to give you inspiration for writing in your book. You return to the crossroads. Now, when you look back up at the mountain, the clouds have cleared and you can see the peak. Soon the white mist fills the space around you once more. When it clears, you are back in the room. Open your eyes when you are ready, ground yourself, and make notes. If you feel moved to do so, try to find a new blank book that resembles the one gifted to you by the sage, in which you can write your faery-inspired creations.

Dance and Movement

One of the most direct modes of expression, connection, and devotion open to us is through the movement of our bodies. Our physical body is not only the vehicle that carries the soul, but it responds to other energies that we sense around and within us. Equally, sometimes the flow of energies can be blocked, especially where intense emotions are concerned, and those tensions can end up stored in the body. By starting with the body and freeing it up as much as possible, allowing those emotions to flow, we can help keep our connections and energy flow clear.

Throughout folklore, art, and literature, faeries and dance have always literally gone hand in hand. A faery dance is thought to be both a beautiful and dangerous thing to behold, always with the edge of fear that if you join the dance, you may never return to your old life. In a symbolic way, this may be true. To dance with Faery is to be transformed, to experience the world in a whole new way, expanding awareness and understanding beyond the usual limits imposed by society.

Dance as a Language

Dance is a universal language—a primal and powerful mode of expression that instinctively carries energy and provokes reaction beyond the cerebral nature of words. Since our connection with the realm of Faery is primarily through the heart rather than the head, dance can help us directly plug into the energies of the inner earth without the intercedence of the rational mind. Of course, the latter should never be completely left behind, but it is important to allow ourselves space and time to simply feel and be with ourselves and our connections.

These experiences may be ephemeral, not thoughts and experiences that can be adequately noted or kept, yet they are all the more potent for that. On the other hand, a sequence of movements may be recalled and used repeatedly for a particular purpose, just as a melody, a phrase, or a sigil might hold an intent or act as a focus, invocation, or even a key to unlock gateways—and if all of the above work for you, why not combine them?

Freeing the Body

Choose a piece of music that moves you emotionally and, if possible, reminds you of some aspect of Faery; for example, harp music might evoke the tale of Thomas the Rhymer. If you can't think of a piece of music, try a drumbeat you can feel through your body that triggers a primal response. You can play this either through speakers or headphones (but obviously be mindful of wires, etc., in the case of the latter). Choose a location either at home or outdoors where you know you won't be disturbed or watched by anyone, as it's important you feel free from fear of judgement. This movement is for you alone at this point.

Stand (or, if you are unable to stand for prolonged periods, sit) in a neutral position with plenty of space around you—at least enough to flail your arms around wildly without knocking over your favourite vase! With your music playing, perform the Faery Tree exercise, drawing energy from below and above into your centre and allowing the music to enter your energetic awareness also.

When the energy meets in your centre, allow that golden light to fill your being and, with it, the music. Which part of your body do you feel it in first? Where are the areas of stiffness or tension? Direct the golden energy to those areas and feel the music, like water in a river, gently but powerfully clearing obstacles. If you are able to move this area, allow it to start to move with the music, and feel it start to release. If you are not able to, allow the energy to flow around it like water to the next part of your body that you can move.

Begin gently. It could simply be a movement of the fingers or a swaying from the hips. How do the combined music and energy move you? Visualise any blockages being either shaken away from the tips of your fingers or flowing down through your feet into the ground. You are a tree and the music is the wind; your roots are deep in the inner earth, feeling the rhythm of Earth's heartbeat. All mundane concerns melt away, emotions are released, and you are a free vessel of expression.

Repeat regularly to keep in touch with your body and maintain it as the best tool for your soul's expression in the world that it can be.

The Dancers on the Water
Guided Visualisation

Sitting upright where you will not be disturbed, close your eyes and take three deep breaths. On each breath out, release all worries and tensions from your everyday life. As you breathe in, a white mist starts to fill your awareness. The mist slowly clears and you find yourself once more at the centre of the crossroads, facing the forest in the north, with the mountain to your right in the east, the desert behind you in the south, and the ocean to your left in the west. This time you are taking the western path down to the water.

The path is winding yet clear, and you move down it at a steady pace. You notice there is a certain rhythm and movement to the path itself, almost as if it were a serpent making its way through the grass, and that movement starts to affect your own rhythm as you find yourself moving at one with the landscape. The sky is a dusky lilac and the long grass around you is scattered with luminous blue flowers that seem to be swaying with their own unified movement as you approach the shore. As you get closer to the water, you realise that the rhythm is that of the waves as they lap gently onto the shore.

The path widens and you walk out onto silver sand. There is a very shallow layer of water over the sand, as if the tide is going out, and the beach acts like a mirror, reflecting the sky above. You notice a pattern of something like footprints leading towards the sea, and you follow these prints, doing your best to follow their pattern. As you do so, it feels natural to place your feet within the prints, moving into a dance as you come to the very edge of the water.

You look up to see three figures somehow dancing on the surface of the water, as if they were made of water themselves, shimmering from within with their own light. They each move in their own way yet are unified. They gesture towards you and you instinctively understand that they mean for you to join them. You find yourself able to do so, temporarily becoming a being of water. As you join them, you become aware of the music and rhythm that is formed of each of their unique notes combining with your own and the rhythm and song of the sea. You allow yourself to move with them as much as feels comfortable for you to do so, expressing your soul's song in unity with theirs. Allow any feelings to surface and flow freely; there may be suppressed energies that need to be released. There is no need to exchange words with these beings, but there is a dialogue of movement between you, a language that is spoken by the heart. Here you can move in ways that are not limited by physical laws or constrictions. All of you will sense together when the time is right to return. In a gesture you convey your gratitude and friendship.

Your body returns to its familiar form as you make your way back up the path towards the crossroads, yet it is somehow freer and looser than it was. You know you can return whenever you wish. When you reach the crossroads, the white mist once more fills your vision. With three deep breaths, the mist disperses and you are back in the room. Feel the weight of your body and refamiliarise yourself gently with your physical form before opening your eyes. Drink and eat something to ground yourself, and make notes if you so wish.

Art, Action, and the Alchemy of Creation

I suppose a less fancy title for this section could be "making stuff with your hands." This covers a very wide range of activities, from creating visual art to baking a pie, but essentially I'm talking about the amazing ability that humans have to manifest something into physical existence from vision and imagination—yes, even (and especially) pie. It is an innate ability that we take for granted, and it is one we can use to strengthen our connection with Faery through completing tasks in this world and manifesting things inspired by their realm into being. Also, as stated earlier in this book, pie makes a *great* offering.

Visionary artists create windows into Faery with their work, feeding our imaginations and helping us build bridges between the realms. On a simpler yet at least as powerful level, sometimes we will receive glyphs, symbols, and sigils in our meditations and journey work that we can then use in this world for whatever purpose they are intended. Our faery allies might also show us tools to find or create or tasks to complete. There will always be work that we need them to do for us in their world and that they need us to do for them in this world. To work with Faery is to be part of a collaborative team, working together towards a greater cause: the balance and health of the world we share.

The Warrior in the Desert
Guided Visualisation

In a place where you know you won't be disturbed, sit comfortably yet upright with your legs uncrossed and close your eyes,
visualising yourself just as you are now in the room. Take three
slow, deep breaths. Breathe out all your daily concerns and allow
tension to melt away from your body. As you breathe in, a white
mist slowly fills your vision. Keeping your breathing steady, the
white mist clears, and you find yourself back at the crossroads.
Before you, to the north, is the forest realm. To your right, in the
east, is the mountain. In the west, to your left, you see the ocean
path, and behind you, in the south, lies the desert. Turn now to
face the southern path.

As you move forward into the desert, you realise how vibrant
and full of life the desert really is. The sky above is a twilight
lilac, the sand beneath your feet is a golden red, with cacti and
other desert plants in full flower all around you in flashes of red

and orange. There is also the occasional tree, adapted to the dry conditions, twisted yet strong. You sense many living creatures around, and though they are elusive, you catch sight of a few animals and faery beings. If any approach you, treat them respectfully and without fear.

As you continue to move forward through this landscape, you realise that one of the shapes in front of you that you thought was a tree is actually a tall figure. They carry a long staff or spear and seem to beckon you forward. You approach the being and see that they are weathered in appearance, with bright, piercing eyes, and their dark body is knotty and strong like the desert trees you mistook them for. They speak:

"Life is creation; creation is life. Sometimes it may feel like that part of us is barren, but just like the desert, life can grow in unexpected ways, in unexpected places. While there is soul, energy, spirit, there is life, creation, joy."

They take their staff and draw a symbol on the ground. Remember this symbol if you can. From the centre of the symbol, a new seedling starts to emerge from the sand. It grows swiftly into a bud, which opens. A small winged being emerges and flies around you in a circle and then off to start its own life. The tall faery being smiles at you, a glimmer in their eye, and passes the staff to you.

You pause for a moment and think about what kind of creativity you would like to bring to the world and how this can build connection with the Faery realm, remembering the symbol that the faery being drew in the sand. You may either replicate their symbol or a new symbol will come to you, and you draw this in the sand. Soon a sapling appears and a bud quickly forms. That bud turns into a bloom, and as it opens, a small orb of bright light emerges from it. It hovers before you, and empathically you understand that it wishes to join you. If you consent, it will join your energy and help you with creative inspiration; otherwise, it will wait until you are ready. Stay with this moment as long as you need to.

When you are ready, thank the tall being, and recall again any symbols you have seen. You understand that you may return whenever you wish and that more symbols may be learned. Bidding farewell, you turn back the way you came and follow the path back towards the crossroads. You feel that colours are somehow brighter, scents are stronger, and a breeze of inspiration is on your back.

You find your way back to the crossroads and the white mist fills your vision once more. As you breathe out, the mist dissipates and you find yourself once more back in the room. Take the time you need until you are ready to open your eyes, and be sure to sketch any symbols you can remember and make any notes. These symbols can be drawn on objects, kept around your home, or used in any way in your work. They will act as keys to help unlock gateways of inspiration within you, which in turn will open doors for others, thus strengthening the bridge between the worlds.

Manifesting the Vision

After taking some time to process your experiences so far, you should have an idea of how your unique contribution to the world may work in relation to Faery. Take some time now to plan and create either an offering to Faery or something dedicated to Faery that will help strengthen your connection. It may be directly inspired by something that you saw, heard, or felt during one of the visualisations or it may be a combination of some or all. It may be very simple; it may be highly complex and time-consuming. It may not be a physical object but a song or dance that is given to the moment. You will have a feeling for what is right and how it should be brought into the world.

Trust your instincts. Now create!

Talicsin (Wales)

Like Thomas the Rhymer, Taliesin was a real historical person who also has this mythologized aspect (his writings may be found online or in published works). This story is taken from the Mabinogion (a significant collection of ancient Welsh tales) and has many similarities with the Irish tale of Fionn Mac Cumhail (or Finn MacCool) and the salmon of wisdom, a tale that also exists in Scotland and the Isle of Man. Again we see the theme of shapeshifting, this time cycling through the different elements, showing that familiarity with (and indeed becoming) earth, water, air, and fire is part of the initiation process...

Far back in the history of the land, there was a man and woman who dwelt in the middle of Lake Tegid in Penllyn. The woman's name was Caridwen and her husband's name was Tegid Voel, and they had two children: a daughter who was the fairest in the land and a son who was the ugliest. Apart from his hideousness, her son, Avagddu, was also unremarkable of mind. Since, like any good mother, she wanted her son to thrive in the world, Caridwen used the knowledge of the ancient alchemist-magicians, the Fferyllt, to create a special brew that would make him the most inspired and gifted mind in the world, both in arts and science.

She put all the ingredients to boil in a cauldron, which at the end of a year and a day would yield but three blessed drops that would grant this wondrous inspiration. Since she could not watch the cauldron herself for all this time, she set Gwion Bach, a young lad from Powys, to stir it, and a blind man, Morda, to keep the fire beneath the cauldron burning. However, after around a year, while Caridwen was busy seeking herbs, three drops sprang from the boiling cauldron and landed on Gwion's finger. He instantly put it in his mouth due to the sharp pain of the scald. As soon as he did so, he was granted the exceptional wisdom and foresight that was meant for Caridwen's son! This same wisdom warned him to be afraid of Caridwen's wrath, so he fled as fast as he could towards his home. As he did so, the cauldron split in two, and all the remaining mixture became toxic and leaked into the river.

● ● ●

Caridwen, furious at the year of wasted work, beat the old blind man until his eye fell out, and he pointed the way that Gwion had fled. Caridwen gave chase, but with Gwion's new knowledge he found that he could take the shape of a hare to outrun her. Caridwen matched him by changing to a greyhound, so Gwion found a river and changed to a fish. Caridwen became an otter to continue the chase, so Gwion became a bird and flew high into the air. Caridwen took the form of a sharp-eyed hawk and pursued him relentlessly until he turned himself into a tiny grain of wheat amongst a whole barn of identical grains, feeling sure that he would now be safely hidden, but Caridwen became a black hen and ate him up! That was not the end of Gwion, however. She bore him for nine months in her womb until he was reborn as a child with a radiant brow. Unable to destroy him because of his beauty, she wrapped him in leather and cast him afloat on the river.

The floating babe was uncovered by Elphin, the son of Gwyddno, who upon seeing the child's beauty named him Taliesin, meaning "radiant brow." The newborn babe instantly started to prophesy good fortune for Elphin, who became a king, and Taliesin grew to become a brilliant poet and visionary, inspiring and bringing sage advice to many.

"Now, ye maun go wi' me," she said,
"True Thomas, ye maun go wi' me:
And ye maun serve me seven years,
Thro' weal or woe as may chance to be."

. . . .

Sir Walter Scott, "Thomas the Rhymer"

Space and Time

Time passes differently in Faery. It's not so much that time doesn't exist, though in many ways it is a timeless land (ah, more contradictions!). It's more as though all of time exists at once, though fluid (not fixed as if fated), and certainly our faery allies have a very different relationship to time than we do, which can lead to some confusion. When working with Faery, always be patient and always be ready, as some things may take a long time, some things may happen quickly, and it may be the things you expected to take a long time will be the ones that happen quickly, and...well, you get the idea.

In folklore and poetry it is well established that if you visit Faery, willingly or unwillingly, many years may pass in the human world when it seemed only a short amount of time in the otherworld. Days become months, months become years; people return to seek their homes and families, only to find the world has moved on without them. This is (probably) not something we need to take too literally, but we should be mindful that we do not neglect our human existence as we immerse ourselves deeper into faery work and thus allow our lives to pass by and neglect our loved ones. It is by living as a human in balance with the world that we are able to best serve our common goals and fulfill our purpose.

The Significance of Seven

Seven is a number which appears regularly in Faery lore and is popularly thought to be a lucky number, though most don't consider why. It is a number deeply tied to the underlying pattern of our existence. We have seven days of the week, which in turn connect to the seven traditional planets, and when we add above, below, and within to the four directions we have already looked at in this book, we have seven directions. In *Faery Craft*, my previous work, I connected these seven directions to the seven points of the septagram (seven-pointed star) and seven qualities that are needed for working with Faery: Knowledge, Connection, Trust, Honour, Magic, Joy, and Inspiration, with Balance at the centre.

Calling On the Seven Directions

You can use the following to help centre yourself at any time (for this purpose it can be done internally as a visualisation if you need to do this where you don't want to be overheard) or as a way of setting up sacred space for any other magical work you have planned. You might also use a version of this to invoke the qualities of the seven directions into any of your creations or offerings. Along with the faery tree, this is a good staple exercise to perform regularly to keep in tune with the energies around you. (This can be adapted for working with a group by replacing "me" with "us" and asking the group to repeat each short phrase after you.)

Begin facing the east. Stand if you are able or sit upright, and raise your arms with palms facing forward. Remember your voice work—the more you are able to resonate and intone these words, the more effective it will be:

> I call to the east and the element of air!
> Grant me your qualities of knowledge,
> clarity, and logic. I ask for the blessings
> of Gorias! Hail and welcome!

Now turn to your right and face the south, arms raised, palms facing forwards:

> I call to the south and the element
> of fire! Grant me your qualities of
> inspiration, will, and action. I ask for the
> blessings of Finias! Hail and welcome!

Now turn again to your right in order to face the west, raising arms and palms forward:

> I call to the west and the element of
> water! Grant me your qualities of joy,
> intuition, and healing. I ask for the
> blessings of Murias! Hail and welcome!

Turn to your right again so that you are now facing the north, arms raised with palms outwards:

**I call to the north and the element of
earth! Grant me your qualities of trust,
stability, and nurture. I ask for the
blessings of Falias! Hail and welcome!**

*Now turn to your right until you are facing the centre of your
space. Raise your dominant arm up to the heavens, looking up
as you call:*

**I call to the above, to the celestial
realm! Grant me connection and
awareness of the divine within all
things. Bless me with your wisdom
and insight! Hail and welcome!**

*Now either crouch and place your hands on the ground or
gesture with palms downwards:*

**I call to the below, to the underworld,
land of the Sidhe and the ancestors.
Grant me your strength and
guidance as I stand on your
shoulders! Hail and welcome!**

Finally, close your eyes and turn your awareness inwards, hands on your heart. If you are in a pair or group, turn inwards to face each other and hold hands:

> **I call to the within, to the star within**
> **each of us. May I walk forward on**
> **this path with honour and balance in**
> **the qualities of all seven directions,**
> **that humanity may once more form**
> **a harmonious constellation with the**
> **inner realms. Hail and welcome!**

When using this exercise to open a space, you should also use it to close at the end of your session, changing the phrasing to "I thank you for the qualities of…", "I thank you for the blessing of…" and adding "hail and farewell" instead of "hail and welcome," moving round the circle, starting in the north and turning left anticlockwise but still finishing with above, below, and within.

The Faery Year

You do not need to belong to any particular religion or spiritual path to work with Faery, but since faery lore is predominantly Celtic (by which I mean the modern use of the word incorporating Irish, Scottish, Welsh, Cornish, and Breton), it is helpful to have some knowledge of the old Celtic festivals, as it is at these times it was thought the worlds were closer together and faery beings most active. These dates are for the Northern Hemisphere, and you may either adapt them, if necessary, to your own location, or look into what equivalent native traditions there are in your area around the shifting of the seasons. The equinoxes and solstices are, of course, an astrological event that applies wherever in the world you are, and there is faery lore attached to these festivals around the world.

Winter Solstice (December 21/22)

The time of year when the night is longest, yet the sun is reborn from the darkness. Different cultures around the world have different names and stories associated with it, but the general theme of celebrating the rebirth of light and life from the darkness is repeated. This is a good time to think about planting seeds of intent for the year ahead. Think about how you would like your Faery work to progress and set some intentions, asking your faery allies for support.

There is a lovely bit of Chinese faery lore that says when a Buddhist emperor forbade his people to eat meat, this displeased the gods, as they liked to feed off the scent of the cooked meat, so they sent a three-year drought. The faery of the cypress tree was sad when she saw people suffering, so she came into the human world as a girl called Jiao and taught people to make meat dumplings as a sacrifice to appease the gods. There is still a tradition of eating dumplings called Jiaozi on the Winter Solstice.

Imbolc (February 1)

Though Imbolc is traditionally celebrated around February 1, I always feel that it is when the first signs of spring appear in the land, which does tend to vary a little. The name comes from "ewe's milk" and is connected to the time when the first lambs are born. Thus it may seem not particularly significant to Faery work, but the power of nature as it rebirths from the dark of winter is apparent at this time, and those beings whose function is to aid that process within the earth are hard at work. In Pagan traditions the goddess Brigid is particularly celebrated at this time, and with her Christian counterpart, Saint Brigid, is associated with wells and the white ladies who are often the spiritual guardians of such places. Therefore, if there is a well or sacred spring near you, or if you have access to one or even if you wish to simply contemplate the power of such a place in meditation, Imbolc is a good time to honour them.

Spring Equinox (March 21/22)

At the equinox the days and nights are of equal length and the sun and moon are in balance with each other, so we can work towards balance in our own lives and between the realms. The Christian festival of Easter (the timing of which depends on the full moon in a rather non-Christian way) tends to fall around this time, and both are concerned with life from death, hope from hopelessness. Working with your faery allies towards peaceful solutions to Earth's conflicts as well as celebrating hope within the world would be beneficial here, and the first shoots of those seeds planted in Samhain should be starting to show.

Beltane (May 1)

Beltane, strongly associated with Mayday, is celebrated at the end of April/beginning of May, but much as with Imbolc, you may prefer to celebrate it when the signs of nature show that spring is fully "sprung." Traditionally this would be when one of the most sacred faery plants, the hawthorn, starts to blossom. This is a festival of love and fertility, so I'm sure you can think of ways you might enjoy celebrating that! Beltane, like its opposite date in the calendar, Samhain, is a most potent time for Faery work. If you wish to make a promise and dedicate yourself seriously to the work, this would be a good time, but take the vow as seriously as you would a marriage. Beltane is a time for dancing and reveling in the primal pleasures of the natural world. It is said that morning dew collected from primroses in the dawn light of Beltane can be splashed on the face to increase beauty, and any spells or charms to draw love into your life are extra charged. Red and white roses and a faery queen in green on a white horse are images to contemplate in your meditations at Beltane.

Summer Solstice (June 20/21)

Summer Solstice, the longest day, is when the sun and thus solar-related forces are most powerful in the world. These days the solstice has become conflated with Midsummer, which is a few days later (around June 24/25). This was an important festival for our ancestors, as it is today, with many still marking the occasion with huge celebrations at monuments such as Stonehenge. It is traditionally a time when faeries might show themselves to humans, perhaps to celebrate the achievements of collaboration over the year. To rise and watch the rising sun in a sacred place at the solstice is a magical experience indeed. It is a time of peak creativity and also a time to banish darkness and negative influences from your life. Use this time to build your connections with Faery, dance, and trust with an open heart, and let them help you keep the shadows at bay. The golden light of the sun setting so late in the day can truly transport you out of time and give you a sense of really stepping into the endless beauty of the primal inner landscape.

Lammas/Lughnasadh (August 1)

This festival is a celebration of the first harvest, and as the Irish name Lughnasadh implies, it is sacred to the ancient Celtic deity

Lugh. Lugh is one of the Tuatha de Danann, known for being tall, youthful, and highly skilled in many disciplines, including smithing, sorcery, swordsmanship, and poetry. He is sometimes equated with Mercury, but his energy is somewhat more fiery and warrior-like. This festival is a time to be thankful for the successes of the year and for the fruits of any collaborative labour you have undertaken with your faery allies. The best part of the harvest would traditionally be offered in gratitude to the spirits of the land and the faery folk, so remember this in your own practice. How can you best express your gratitude? Have your allies helped you with any skills that you could now turn to in creating an offering for them? Reflect on the achievements of the year so far. Looking back at where you started, rejoice in your victories and give thanks.

Autumn Equinox (September 21/22)

Once again, the day and night are of equal length, but now it is giving way slowly to the long nights of winter as the warmth and life retreat from the world. This is a good time for journaling and reflecting back on the year and seeing what lessons have been learned. In what ways have you worked towards balance in your faery work and your daily life? How can you achieve better balance and perhaps help others do the same? Spend time in peace and contemplation of the sunset, notice the ways in which nature starts to wind down and prepare for winter, and consider how you might do the same. Note how the trees start to lose their leaves but the beauty of the colours that foretell that loss and the knowledge of the cycle that is to continue all must give way to loss in order to be reborn again in spring. When we experience loss, it can feel as though that grief will be with us forever, but our friends in nature can show us that there is always life and hope to come.

Samhain (October 31)

Pronounced *sow-ihn*, this festival marks the end of harvest and the beginning of winter. Traditionally a time of introspection, remembering ancestors and those who have passed, the veil between worlds is thin at this time, which means that not only are the spirits of the dead closer to us, but so is the faery realm. The much-feared Wild Hunt is said to ride out at this time, led by the king of Faery and the underworld, followed by baying hounds and the fiercest of faery beings and accompanied by storms and winds; it is advised for all mortal folk to avoid them! It is, however, a potent time for deep Faery work and a good time for underworld journeys and offerings.

This date is more popularly celebrated as Halloween, and there is certainly no harm in dressing up in a faery-inspired outfit to celebrate with friends before returning home for more meditative practices. Faeries approve of fun so long as it is respectful, and the act of changing one's appearance can be transformative and transporting in surprising ways.

The Moon

Within the grand cycle of the wheel of the year, there are many smaller cycles of life, death, and rebirth, ruled by the waxing and waning of the moon. The moon is our window into magic and the otherworld and is intrinsically linked to our work with Faery. The sun rules over science, logic, and the conscious, visible world, and the moon rules over the unseen, the mystical, and the watery depths of the subconscious. In the time of our ancestors, the day was for human life and the night was for the faery folk, whose circle dance you might catch a glimpse of if you were brave enough to walk in the forest by moonlight. Now we light the night by artificial means, bringing the sun's science into the moon's domain and limiting our contact with enchantment. However, the cycle of the moon still affects us, mostly water as we are, and we feel her pull on our inner tides whether we see her or not.

The Moon and Her Faery Queens

Many goddesses of the moon also count faery queen amongst their titles, most notably Diana, who in Renaissance times was also considered Queen of the Witches, along with her fellow faery queen, Hekate. Shakespeare even took the name for his faery queen, Titania, from one of the titles of Diana that relates to her nature as a daughter of Titans, the race of mighty deities that ruled before the Olympian gods in Greek mythology. Both Diana and Hekate are goddesses connected to the world soul, a platonic philosophical and mystical concept that we looked at in relation to Faery earlier in this book. The moon was considered the seat of the world soul. It is through the moon that soul/energy/spirit is conveyed from the ultimate universal source into the world. With our faery queen goddesses as personifications of this world soul and faery beings as sparks of this divine energy, a whole philosophical picture may be formed from which we may gain mystical understanding.

Moon Meditation

Although this meditation is written to work as a guided visuali-sation, it would be most effective if you are able to get to a moon-lit body of water to perform it.

Choose a night with a clear sky to perform this meditation. If you are able to see the moon and be touched by her light, either via a window or out in nature, that is ideal. Sit comfort-ably, legs uncrossed, in a place where you will not be disturbed. Close your eyes and visualise yourself and your surroundings as you are now. If you do have moonlight upon you, see if you can sense it and how it affects your energy and the room around you. Take three deep breaths in and out. As you breathe out, all your daily concerns are exhaled away. As you breathe in, a white mist fills your vision. On another three deep breaths, each breath out clears the mist, and you find yourself on a beach at night. The sky is clear, the stars are bright overhead, and there is a full moon directly ahead of you, over the ocean. If there is a beach that you have visited in reality that you can picture strongly, this will help you. Spend some time taking in the scene with all your senses. Feel the sand wet beneath your feet; feel a cool breeze. The sea is calm, but you can hear the gentle lapping of the waves and see the silver light of moon and stars reflected on its surface.

After spending some time relaxing and taking in the peaceful majesty of the scene, you notice that there seems to be a star directly above the moon that shines brighter than all the others, brighter even than a planet might. As you shift your focus to this star, you notice that there is a ray of light shining directly down to the moon, and as you observe it, it is growing in brightness. When the light reaches the moon, it is as though the moon is a prism, the light refracting downwards into a silvery ray that hits at the full spectrum. As this light continues to expand outwards from the moon, the night sky is transformed into a swirling spectrum of colour with the moon at its centre.

After a few minutes, this spectrum of light resolves itself into a path that leads from the moon down onto the surface of the water in front of you. Emerging from the moon, as if it were a gateway, descends a female figure clad in white with a crescent on her forehead. As she stands before you, you salute her respectfully by placing your hands in prayer position to your heart, your lips, and then your forehead. While she is standing before you, shimmering with her own light, which is also that of the Moon, you are able to notice more detail. She carries a pair of torches, with a key around her neck and a knife on a belt around her waist.

Which of these objects are you most drawn to? You may ask her a question about this object, and she may answer you. She may also choose to give this object to you. See if an object appears in your hands to exchange, and consider what this may symbolise in terms of service or offerings. Give time for this encounter to unfold as it will.

When your exchange comes to a natural conclusion, give respectful thanks and bid farewell. She will ascend once more up the pathway into the Moon. The light will slowly cease its swirling and the night sky will return to its previous state. The white mist reappears to fill your vision, and when it clears, you are back in the room where you started. When you are ready, open your eyes, readjust to your body, and make any notes you wish to make. Be sure to ground yourself with a bite to eat and a drink of water or by your own preferred method.

Full Moon Activity Suggestions

At the full moon our emotions often can be at their wildest and our dreams at their weirdest, but our creativity is also at its peak! It's also the best time to leave offerings for both faery and spirits of place. Here are some suggestions for how to best use full moon energy:

- If you can, go out into nature under moonlight and leave an offering in a place that is special to you.

- Perform the Faery Tree exercise and see how it feels different by moonlight.

- What type of creative act are you most drawn to: Painting? Writing? Dancing? Singing? See if you can create a piece dedicated to faery in your chosen medium.

- If you have a view of the moon from your home, take time to leave the curtains open and simply bathe in her light, letting her recharge your magical self.

- If you have any tools you use in your work, these can be charged by the light of the full moon.

Waning Moon Activity Suggestions

As the moon wanes and the tide of power ebbs, it is a good time to clear out and banish things from our lives that have outstayed their welcome. Here are some suggestions for activities to undertake during the waning and dark moon:

- Are there any bad habits you would like to break? Either write them out or draw a sigil (a simple symbol) that represents them, ask your faery allies for help in forming better habits, and burn the paper.

- If you are keeping a shrine for your Faery work, the waning moon is a good time to make sure it is clean and clear from debris. Also, you could take a bag out into your local parks or sites in nature that you visit and clear it of litter.

- Likewise, cleaning your house with magical intent during this time can create space for new, positive energy to come in!

- If there are old relationships or friendships that have become toxic but the shadow of influence still remains, ask your faery allies to help you cut the emotional cords that bind you so you can be free. This can be represented with a physical cord cut in sacred space with magical intent and also done in meditation with the help of your allies.

Dark Moon Divination

The dark of the moon is the best time of the month to work with your faery allies on divination. There are many wonderful faery-inspired tarot and oracle decks out there (including my own *Tarot of the Sidhe*), most of which come with their own instruction book, so this is a great place to start.

Other methods you could try include:

- Scrying, either in water or a dark mirror. Instruction is advised from an experienced teacher. Stare at the reflective surface and allow images to form, but do not leave the surface uncovered and unattended.

- Dice. See Stephen Ball's excellent *Elemental Divination* (Llewellyn, 2019) for a system that works very well in conjunction with Faery teachings.

- Runes. Those drawn to the Alfar and Nordic beliefs will find these most resonant.

- Natural patterns and omens. Observe the world around you and look for signs. Ask your faery allies for help in interpreting the symbols around you and also look to folklore. Birds, clouds, leaves that fall—anything can be interpreted within the framework of divination.

New Moon Activity Suggestions

As you might imagine, new moon, new energies, new plans! Here are some suggestions for activities to undertake once the first sliver of the new crescent shows:

- Start a journal for your Faery work, if you haven't already, and set goals and intentions for the month ahead.

- How about planting some literal seeds? Planting wildflowers in particular is a wonderful act of service to nature and Faery.

- Have you been waiting for a good time to start a Faery-related project? New moon is a good time to get the ball rolling, even if it's just jotting down plans.

- Is there a location that you've wanted to visit but haven't yet found time? See if you can make time at a new moon to forge those new energetic connections.

- Contemplate the crescent of the new moon as a symbol of rebirth. Spend time meditating upon it, breathing in hope and good intentions for the month ahead.

- Start to learn a new skill that might benefit your Faery work, such as learning an instrument, baking, or working on your creative arts.

Waxing Moon Activity Suggestions

As the moon is waxing, the seeds planted at the new moon will continue to grow. Here are some other suggestions for activities that would fit with the energy of a waxing moon as it builds towards full:

- Build existing connections and relationships and continue to work on existing skills.

- Keep learning! Research folklore and read versions of myths related to Faery lore that speak to you. How might this knowledge be incorporated into your work?

- When the moon is half full, contemplate the balance of energies in your life. Do you give time for stillness as well as movement and reflection as well as action?

- How can you help others grow in their awareness and relationship to the natural realm?

- Make sure that new projects keep up momentum. Remind yourself to keep writing in your journal and maintain relationship with your faery allies.

- Start to plan a potential creative project for the next full moon.

- Do you practice any form of energy healing? See if your faery allies can help you use your new connections to enhance this skill. They also can help you find new allies who specialise in healing.

Deepening Connection with Your Ally/Allies

Like any relationship, once you have established contact with your otherworldly allies, work and attention are required to keep the connection healthy and establish trust between you. Once you have connected with your first ally, they can help you find both Faery and animal spirits in the otherworld who will be specialised in certain areas. Once you have started working in earnest, you may also find that it works the other way around and that they start to seek you out. You will find that just as in the human world, faery beings have different roles that they fulfill and work that they perform. There are teachers, guides, warriors, artists, healers, and prophets, many of whom may be willing to help you with your work, and you in turn will be able to help them by acting in our world. It must always be a respectful and collaborative relationship.

Keep Journeying

The underworld journey is a powerful way to keep your connection with your faery allies strong and to meet and learn from other allies they can introduce you to. Try the different ways of journeying suggested in chapter 3, "The Road to Faery"; e.g., if the drum sound doesn't work for you, try waves, white noise, or simply silence (perhaps even noise-canceling headphones) or also using the Great Glyph of the Sidhe as a gateway. Once you have established contact with an ally or guide, they will be there to meet you at your starting point. Don't journey without a clear intent, though! Here are some ideas to get you started:

- Find out more about your ally if they are willing (but respect their privacy if they are not). For example, is there an ancestral connection to you or are they connected to a particular place? What work do they wish to pursue with you? Why were they drawn to work with you in particular? Remember, these are real beings with their own existences! If they are attached to a particular location, ask if they have any names or symbols associated with them that you can wear about you to keep the bond strong.

- Ask about the location where you live. There may be work you can do together to heal trauma on the land or clear blockages. Are there any energy centres or lines there to be found and worked with?

- Ask for help and inspiration with any connected skills you are working on developing or talents you already have that you wish to dedicate to Faery.

- Ask your ally to help you learn how to use land energies in healing work for yourself, the land, and others.

- Journey to find sigils for different purposes, such as healing, unlocking gateways, protection, etc. One at a time, though!

- Your faery ally can also help you face and integrate your shadow self once you have a good and trusting working relationship.

Remember, self-knowledge is key. Always look for ways you can improve your awareness of your nature and impact on the world.

Keep Up the Basics

Simple is sometimes best, and even in a busy life we can make time for basic exercises. Ten minutes a day is better than a whole day once a year, much like physical exercise! Here are your core simple practices to keep up:

- Faery tree exercise. Of course this is best outside, but even in your living room this will help keep you connected and your energy flowing.

- Your true note. Even if you think you don't have a strong voice, it doesn't matter. Let it be free! Release fear! Your voice and connection with faery and your own inner power will grow together.

- Offerings really can be as simple as an apple or a song every full moon.

- Simply be in nature as much as possible, alone, and allow yourself to be still, silent, and receptive. Notice the shifts of energy and the changes in the landscape with the seasons.

Keep Creating

Everyone has the potential to be creative, and if you feel self-conscious about it, no one has to see but yourself. Making time for writing, art, singing, dancing, knitting, baking…any or all of these things will keep you open to the inspiration offered by Faery. See how you might incorporate symbols, places, beings, and other experiences you have had into your creations.

Embrace Change

As I said at the top of this chapter, Faery is both timeless and yet experiences all of time at once. It is constant yet fluid and ever shifting. Faery beings are often shapeshifters and thus are agents of transformation within our lives. Sometimes it can seem as though the change is chaotic—systems are shaken up, foundations tested, false structures (that we are often very attached to) are stripped away. This can be an uncomfortable process, but if we are able to embrace it and see the inner purpose behind it—if we can flow around obstacles and learn to be shapeshifters ourselves—it can be an exhilarating journey!

With this in mind, be aware that sometimes our allies will change; they may stay with us forever or they may move on and others take their place. Just like earthly companions, sometimes our paths take us in different directions. Sometimes it may be the same ally, but they might seem changed themselves, taking on a different appearance or even a different name. Well, don't people change too? Sometimes we have to adapt and deal with difficult change in our own lives and (as in my own case) have to move away from places and allies we have worked to build a close connection with. Hold onto trust. New connections may take time, but you are where you are and who you are in this moment for a reason. Perhaps I would not have the insight into this particular challenge if I was not facing it myself, and through that, perhaps those are the words you needed to read. As I said earlier, you are unique. We are all unique. And yet, in another seeming contradiction, we are all connected. We are all part of a greater existence that encompasses both humanity and Faery. We are all one.

The Sleeping Warriors (Europe)

The sleeping warriors myth occurs throughout Europe, and while there are some variants (in most places the king is Arthur, but in Ireland, Scotland, and some other places, it is Finn MacCool), the tale remains the same…

Deep under the green hills, hidden from mortal sight, lie a great king and his warriors, not dead but sleeping, awaiting for one to awaken them when the time is right for them to return to the world in its greatest need. This had been known for many hundreds of years, but none had found the entrance to where they lay until one day a shepherd who sat knitting on top of the mound dropped his ball of yarn, and he followed it as it rolled down a deep, narrow hole.

Cutting his way through the thick thorns that covered the hole, he followed his wool down into a long, dark, narrow passageway, with a light shining at the far end. Thinking that he must have found the legendary sleepers (or perhaps some treasure), he followed the light until the passageway opened into a large chamber. There, to his wonder, he found the sleeping king, his queen, and his warriors. The light was coming from a fire burning in the hearth, in front of which were sleeping dozens of hunting dogs. Also in front of the fire were a horn, a stone sword, and a garter. The shepherd drew the sword and all the sleeping company began to stir. He used the sword to cut the garter, and the king, queen, and knights looked as though they were about to rise, but afraid of what was happening, the shepherd replaced the sword, and all the sleeping figures returned to their slumber, apart from the king, who, before he fell once more to rest, raised his hands and intoned in a terrible voice:

> "O woe betide that evil day
> On which the witless wight was born
> Who drew the sword—the garter cut—
> But never blew the bugle horn!"

● ● ●

It is an appealing thought to take this myth literally and hope that we may still awaken the sleepers and that they will return and save us from the dire mess we've made of the planet. And the truth is, we can wake them…for they are us. Within us all are the sleeping warriors that must be awoken, and time is running short.

Conclusion

Thank you for taking this trip into Faery; I feel honoured to have been able to accompany you on your first steps. The world is in a state of apparent chaos and crisis. It seems there is little time for the old ways, yet more than ever we need to strengthen the connection between our worlds. By working on ourselves and reconnecting with the hidden realms that were so important to our ancestors, we can bring forth positive change. It can be overwhelming seeing where the world is apparently heading and feeling powerless to do anything about it, but one person changing might perhaps be a beacon of hope to others. One person making changes and doing work in the inner realms that helps to heal and influence the outer? That's not nothing. That is something very tangible. And you are not alone.

Now you stand at the crossroads, your ally by your side, and where you go from here is up to you. If you do choose to go further on this path, you may choose to dedicate yourself formally and make a promise that must not be taken lightly. Of course you may use your own words, but here is one version for you to use or be inspired by, as you wish:

A Vow to Faery

By the moon above and the stars beneath my feet,
I will walk with honour in both worlds,
Weaving a path that is both my own and yours.
I will listen to your whispers on the wind,
And my own song will join them.
Together we will build a bridge
To balance, to harmony, to a green land of hope;
May what was torn asunder be fixed anew,
May promises that were broken be reforged with inner strength,
May my heart be ever open and the trust between us never wane
While breath is in me and light is within the land.
This I vow, by earth and air, water and fire
In honour, in truth, and in love.

A Blessing

And these words now, from me to you…
By the silver light of the moon and stars
And by the green light of the inner realm
By the great ocean's tide, which flows and ebbs
By the four winds and their graces be bless'd!
Wander deep along the forest path and
Know the light within will always guide you.
May your open heart sing your soul's true note
And may the shining ones who hear its song
Know you and welcome you as an old friend.
In health, in truth, in love, and in friendship,
Blessings of the hidden realm upon you!

Recommended Readings and Teachings

To help you with further learning and adventuring, here are some suggestions to take you deeper:

R. J. Stewart

If you're not already familiar with his work, pay a visit to R. J. Stewart's website. Not only does he have a great body of work available in his books, but he also offers courses. I recommend starting with *The Living World of Faery* and *The Well of Light*.

https://rjstewart.org/

John and Caitlín Matthews

John and Caitlín Matthews have written well over a hundred books on Arthurian myth, shamanic practices, Grail mysteries, mystical practices, and Faery lore. Again, a rich body of work, so rather than point you to one book in particular, visit their site and see what you are drawn to. For this particular subject matter, do make sure you get a copy of John's *The Sidhe: Wisdom from the Celtic Otherworld*.

http://www.hallowquest.org.uk/

Brian and Wendy Froud

Brian Froud is best known for his work as conceptual designer on the fantasy movies *Labyrinth* and *Dark Crystal*, and Wendy was one of the creators of the original Yoda puppet in the *Star Wars* movies, but though they are known for fantasy, both are very much visionary artists with true sight of the Faery realm and have a number of books and oracle decks that are rich with both wisdom and lore.

Katharine Briggs

No faery library is complete without the seminal works of Katharine Briggs, to which many modern writers on the subject owe a huge debt! See if you can find copies of A *Dictionary of Fairies* (Penguin Books, 1976) and *The Fairies in Tradition and Literature* (1967).

Walter Evans-Wentz

In the early years of the twentieth century, Evans-Wentz toured Celtic lands collecting folkloric accounts directly from people who had either encountered faeries or had heard stories passed down by parents and grandparents. This extraordinary collection of knowledge is readily available as *The Faery Faith in Celtic Countries* (1911).

The Secret Commonwealth of Elves, Fauns and Fairies

First published in 1815, this real-life account of Faery contact was written by the Reverend Robert Kirk in the late seventeenth century and discovered upon his death in 1692.

Faery Craft and Tarot of the Sidhe

By me. Please do check out my other work. *Faery Craft* (Llewellyn, 2012) covers some of the same ground as this book but is more focused on lifestyle. It also has some different exercises and interviews with people from the Faery community, including artists, authors, musicians, and teachers. *Tarot of the Sidhe* (Schiffer, 2011) was a channeled work designed not only for divination but to act as a bridge between worlds, so even if you don't want a tarot for readings, the images can help access the realm of the Sidhe.

Acknowledgments

Firstly, thanks to my editor Angela Wix for suggesting this project to me and being very patient as various factors delayed the process. Thanks to my partner, fellow Llewellyn author Stephen Ball, who enthusiastically read every little segment as I sent it, even when he was trying to work himself. Thanks as always to my Gothspring, who puts up with their mum being forever busy with several things at once and is still a faery child deep down.

Eternal gratitude to John and Caitlín Matthews for their work and inspiration over the years, not least to John for introducing me to the Great Glyph of the Sidhe, and also to R. J. Stewart, who also inspires greatly as one who truly walks the paths. Thanks also to my dear friend Sorita D'Este for all the magic, laughter, and encouragement over the years.

To Ellen Kushner, Delia Sherman, and all in the "All the Bard's Words" group who have been a huge moral support over the crazy year that has been 2020 and so encouraging of my writing and esoteric ramblings!

To all those who were involved in my first book on the subject, *Faery Craft*, I hope you'll find work of worth here to build on those foundations.

Thanks to all supporters on my Patreon! If you want to join them for exclusive content, occasional rambles, and sneak previews, it's patreon.com/emilycarding.

To all those in the unseen realms who guide and inspire, timeless gratitude and peace to you.

Bibliography

Briggs, Katharine. 1976. A *Dictionary of Fairies*.
Middlesex, UK: Penguin Books.

Carding, Emily. 2012. *Faery Craft*. Woodbury, MN:
Llewellyn.

D'Este, Sorita, ed. 2012. *The Faerie Queens*. London:
Avalonia Books.

Evans-Wentz, W. Y. 2006. *The Faery Faith in Celtic
Countries*. West Valley City, UT: Waking Lion Press.

Gregory, Lady. 2006 [1904]. *Gods and Fighting Men*.
Norfolk, UK: Colin Smythe.

Hawken, Paul. 1976. *The Magic of Findhorn*. NY:
Fontana.

James I and Brett R. Warren, trans., ed. 2016 [1597]. *The
Annotated Daemonologie*. Unknown: Brett Warren.

Kirk, Robert. 2008 [1691]. *The Secret Commonwealth
of Elves, Fauns and Fairies*. Mineola, NY: Dover
Publications.

Macleod, Fiona. 1913. *At the Turn of the Year: Essays and Nature Thoughts.* Edinburgh, UK: Turnbull and Spears.

Matthews, John. 2004. *The Sidhe: Wisdom from the Celtic Otherworld.* Issaquah, WA: The Lorian Association.

Rankine, David. 2009. *The Book of Treasure Spirits.* London: Avalonia Books.

Rossetti, Christina. 1862. "Goblin Market." https:// www.poetryfoundation.org/poems/44996/ goblin-market.

Russell, George William. 1918. *The Candle of Vision.* London: Macmillan and Co.

Scott, Sir Walter. 1802. "Thomas the Rhymer." https://www.poemhunter.com/poem/thomas-the -rhymer-3/.

Stewart, R. J. 1995. *The Living World of Faery.* Lake Toxaway, NC: Mercury Publishing.

Yeats, W. B. 1889. "The Stolen Child" in *The Wanderings of Oisin and Other Poems.* London: Paul, Trench & Co.

Siolo Thompson (Seattle, WA) is a visual artist and author who employs multiple techniques and narrative forms, from traditional painting to comics and sequential illustration. Her work has been published and exhibited worldwide.

© Roxanna Walitzki